Published in 2009 by Prion
An imprint of the Carlton Publishing Group
20 Mortimer Street
London W1T 3JW

10 9 8 7 6 5 4 3 2 1

A CIP catalogue record for this book is available from the
British Library.

ISBN 978 1 85375 719 8

Printed and bound in the UK by CPI Mackays ME5 8TD

THE
MINI
MISCELLANY

Fifty years of facts, figures, stories and oddities
featuring the world's greatest little car

**GEOFF
TIBBALLS**

PRION

❖ Note on currency ❖

The UK system of pounds, shillings and pence (£ s d), with 20 shillings to the pound and 12 pence to the shilling, was replaced by decimal currency in 1971. One shilling (1s) became 5p and one penny (1d) became roughly 0.5p.

❖ Introduction ❖

Our first family car was a Mini. My Dad, who didn't learn to drive until he had turned forty, bought her around 1962. Her name was Ada (in honour of her Hastings registration ADY), she was Speedwell Blue in colour, and the freedom and adventure she brought us after years of travel on Southern Region trains, Maidstone & District buses and Green Line coaches was immeasurable. Overnight, we had access to the beauty of the English countryside as Ada pootled merrily along winding lanes, affording us views of oast houses and village cricket matches that had previously been visible only through smoky carriage windows. She regularly made the journey up the A21 to London and even transported us to such far flung lands as Sunderland when we visited friends. And she never once complained.

Ada stayed with us through most of the 1960s before eventually being replaced by a less charismatic 1100. My Dad had numerous cars after that but none have remained fondly in the memory. As the adverts said, 'You never forget your first Mini' – even if you weren't actually old enough to drive it at the time.

Since Ada first nipped around the highways and byways of the Home Counties, over five million Minis have been sold; 2009 marks the fiftieth birthday of

Alec Issigonis's revolutionary little car and, although production of the classic Mini ceased in 2000, the anniversary is being marked by celebrations across the world, including Australia, New Zealand, the United States, Malaysia and, of course, the UK.

Named 'Car of the Century' by *Autocar*, the Mini epitomised the Swinging Sixties, both on the road and race track. Dancing through rush-hour traffic, zipping around Brands Hatch, or tackling treacherous Alpine hairpins en route to Monte Carlo – just about anything was possible with a Mini. It was a classless car, one driven by celebrities and plumbers alike – from Peter Sellers to cistern sellers. And judging by the affection in which it is still held, there is plenty of mileage left in the good old Mini yet.

Geoff Tibballs, 2009

THE
MISCELLANY

'Remember the impact this little car had in 1959. The surprise of everyone at a responsible lot like BMC putting their famous Austin and Morris labels on a comic creation whose engine faced the wrong way; had tiny wheels, no drive-shaft down the middle and rubber springs.' – *The Motor*, 1964

❖ From Riches to Rags ❖

Alec Issigonis was born in 1906 in Smyrna (modern day Izmir), a city which historically veered between Turkish and Greek rule, although then, as now, it was part of Turkey. His father, Constantine, was Greek by birth but had subsequently acquired British nationality while absenting himself from the family's highly successful marine engineering business. Turkey sided with Germany in the First World War, and although Constantine's wife was German, his British nationality (allied to his refusal to allow his factory to work for the German navy) resulted in the Issigonis family being placed under house arrest and their property confiscated. After the war, Smyrna was handed over to Greece, but within two years a Turkish uprising saw the city burned to the ground, and all British citizens – including the Issigonises – were evacuated.

Their first port of call was Malta, where they were forced to live as refugees in a tented village. Worse still, Constantine fell ill and died shortly afterwards. In 1923, Alec and his mother, Hulda, arrived in London. Alec's first car was a Singer, in which he chauffeured his mother around Europe in 1925 in what he later described as a 'never-ending succession of breakdowns'. That dismal experience encouraged him to enrol on a three-year engineering course at Battersea Polytechnic, where he failed the maths exam three times but excelled at drawing. Later attempting to justify this academic blind spot, he explained: 'All creative people hate mathematics. It's the most uncreative subject you can study.'

He entered the motor trade as a designer and engineer for Humber in Coventry, where he worked primarily on developing new forms of independent suspension, before being taken on by Morris at their Cowley, Oxford, plant in 1936 under the leadership of Leonard Lord. During the Second World War, Issigonis worked on a number of strange projects for Morris, including a motorised wheelbarrow that could be dropped in a cylinder by parachute and then assembled on the ground. He also planned an amphibious version, which had four wheels and oars for propulsion on water, but neither made it to production.

In 1943, he began work on the design of a small car codenamed 'Mosquito', and five years later, at London's first post-war Motor Show, it was unveiled as the Morris Minor, which went on to become the first British car to sell a million.

After a spell at Alvis, he rejoined BMC – and Lord – in 1955, this time at the Austin plant at Longbridge, Birmingham. Issigonis said he was pleased to be reunited with his old boss whom he described as 'a tough, wonderful man with a fantastic personality, a born businessman and a great production engineer.'

❖ A Fresh Approach ❖

'One thing that I learned the hard way – well not the hard way, the easy way – is when you're designing a new car for production, never, never, copy the opposition.' – Alec Issigonis

❖ From the Bubble to the Orange Box ❖

Designed as project ADO15 (Austin Drawing Office project number 15), the Mini came about because of a fuel shortage. In 1956, as a result of the Suez Crisis which reduced oil supplies, the United Kingdom saw the re-introduction of petrol rationing. Sales of large cars slumped, and there was a boom in the market for so-called Bubble cars.

Mainly West German in origin, Bubble cars such as the Messerschmitt, Heinkel, Glas Goggomobil, and BMW's Isetta – the last-named described by one writer as 'a strange device like an Easter egg mounted on a roller skate' – had a front-entry door, two seats and a noisy motorcycle-derived engine. To save costs, the Isetta had no reverse gear, which meant that drivers who took advantage of small parking spaces by parking front-end-on to the kerb or close to a wall were often unable to open the door. Instead they had to make an ignominious exit by climbing out through the folding canvas sunroof.

Leonard Lord, the somewhat autocratic head of BMC, decreed that something had to be done quickly. He was reported to have said: 'God damn these bloody awful Bubble cars. We must drive them off the road by designing a proper miniature car.'

He laid down some basic design requirements: the car should be contained within a box that measured 10 × 4 × 4 feet (3 × 1.2 × 1.2 m); and the passenger accommodation should occupy six feet (1.8 m) of the 10 foot (3 m) length; and the engine, for reasons of cost, should be an existing unit. Alec Issigonis, with his skills in designing small cars, was a natural for the task.

The team that designed the Mini was remarkably small: as well as Issigonis, there was Jack Daniels (who had worked with him on the Morris Minor), Chris Kingham (who had been with him at Alvis), two engineering students and four draughtsmen. Together, by October 1957, they had designed and built the original prototype, which was affectionately named 'The Orange Box' because of its colour.

⌖ Watching His Weight ⌖

'Issigonis knew what he wanted and made sure he got it. He'd come round holding an ounce weight and say, "Have you saved that for me today?" Weight was very critical. The Mini had to be 10 feet long – no more, no less. He was very pedantic like that and very domineering. When it went into production, it was a quarter of an inch over 10 feet long. That really annoyed him.' – John Sheppard, BMC engineer

⌖ From Charwoman to Chairman ⌖

For many years, Issigonis had visualised creating what he called a 'charwoman's car', a vehicle that would be affordable to a cleaner and a pleasure for her to drive. In July 1958, his vision – in the form of the prototype XC/9003 – was tested by BMC chairman Leonard Lord around the inner roads at Longbridge. Issigonis later recounted how Lord drove at breakneck speed for five minutes before screeching to a halt outside the main door.

As he climbed from the car, slightly dazed, Lord simply ordered: 'Build it!'

Lord wanted the car delivered within 12 months, and when Issigonis protested that such a tight timescale would be expensive, the chairman replied:

'Don't worry about the money. I shall sign the cheques. You get on with getting the thing to work.'

❖ Keeping It Small ❖

Following Leonard Lord's stipulation that the new car should be of the minimum size necessary to accommodate four people, Alec Issigonis took four wooden chairs, arranged them on the Longbridge workshop floor in two rows, and sat down four members of his team. The chairs were then moved around, the personnel changed, until it was generally agreed that the minimum space had been achieved. At that point, chalk lines were drawn on the floor to illustrate the desired dimensions, and these were then measured.

John Cutler, a member of the design team, recalled: 'The designs originated from putting seats on the shop floor. Then we got all sorts of people to sit on them – secretaries from the offices, 6ft manual workers – and we got them to indicate what space they needed in the car. We measured how much space would be needed to open a map, where a pocket would be needed to stow the map. It is a very ergonomic car.'

To provide space for four people, Issigonis devoted 80 per cent of the car's 10-foot (3m) length to passengers and luggage, which left him with around 18 inches (46cm) to accommodate the engine and the gearbox. By turning the engine sideways and mounting the gearbox beneath it in the oil sump, he managed to squeeze everything in.

❖ Name Change ❖

In its early stages of development, the Mini was referred to as the Austin Newmarket, partly because it was aimed at a new market and also because at the time BMC liked to name its cars after places – hence the Somerset, Westminster and Cambridge.

❖ Hand Built by Albert ❖

The first Mini from the Longbridge plant was built by foreman Albert Green, virtually entirely by hand. The order had come from above to build three prototype Minis but with the workforce busy on the plant's other three lines – making Westminsters, A40s and A35 vans – Green decided on a bold course of action. He appointed his chief inspector, Freddie Finch, as inspector for the entire Mini assembly line and, using a selection of borrowed tools, set about building the car by himself. Placing all the components for the three Minis along the 220 yards (200 metres) of the assembly line, he started at one end and worked his way to the other, with Finch monitoring the work at every stage. Amazingly, everything fitted together perfectly and seven hours later, Green had the honour of driving that first Mini off the production line.

'A Bloody Mess!'

When George Harriman, who had succeeded Leonard Lord as managing director of BMC, saw the first pre-production Mini in the Longbridge shop, all polished and ready to go, he was not impressed. 'What a bloody mess!' he exclaimed to Issigonis. 'We'll never sell that. Spend another few quid on it Alec, and jazz it up a bit. Put some chrome plate on it or something.' So they added wheel discs and a chrome strip around the wings.

Austin and Morris

Although it entered public consciousness as the Mini, the new car was officially called the Austin Seven (or Se7en as it was often advertised) if built at Longbridge or the Morris Mini Minor if built at Cowley. The two factories were about 60 miles apart, and in those days there was no major road network connecting them, the M40 and M42 motorways not being completed until the 1990s.

It was not until the start of 1962 that the Austin Seven became known as the Austin Mini. Apart from the name, the only differences between the Austin and Morris versions were the grilles, badges and colour ranges. For the first three years, Austins were available in Speedwell Blue, Tartan Red and Farina Grey, while the Morris came in Clipper Blue, Cherry Red and Old English White. Finally in 1969, the separate Austin and Morris badges were dropped altogether, and the car was marketed simply as the Mini.

❖ Reduce Speed Now! ❖

With a 948cc engine, the 'Orange Box' had a top speed of 92mph, which seemed excessive since most small cars of the time could barely manage 70mph.

The eventual production model differed from the 'Orange Box' by the addition of a front subframe, on which the engine was mounted, and by the engine being mounted with the carburettor at the back, rather than at the front as it had been in the prototype. The change in position, which was to combat the threat of carburettor icing in cold weather, required an extra gear to be placed between engine and transmission. And by lowering the engine capacity to 848cc, the car's top speed was reduced to a more desirable level. The only drawback with moving the engine around was that it exposed the distributor to water coming in through the grille.

❖ The Vision of Issigonis ❖

'I thought we had to do something better than the bubble cars. I thought we should make a very small car for the housewife that was economical to run with lots of shopping space inside which didn't need a big boot.' – Alec Issigonis

❖ Teething Troubles ❖

One of the early Mini prototypes was soon taken for a test run by the plant's Chief Development Engineer Gil Jones who subsequently produced a five-page report listing the car's defects. He noted that the clutch was impossible to disengage, the steering column was in the wrong place, there was a grating noise in the gears, the water pump squealed, and the handbrake only locked the offside wheel.

Furthermore, a number of items had simply not been fitted properly. Jones reported that the doors and rear number plate rattled, the sun visor was 'loose on its hinges and falling down', the petrol pump was wrongly positioned, the radiator was too high, the accelerator pedal was too short, and the self-cancelling trafficator did not self-cancel.

Apart from that, everything was fine!

❖ Wizardry on Wheels ❖

The Mini was formally launched on August 26, 1959. The newspaper advertisements that day ran: 'You've never seen a small car like this before. Front-wheel drive. Fully independent suspension. Up to 50mpg. Over 70mph. And that's only the beginning…. Ten feet long, but roomier inside than many an £800 saloon.' They went on: 'All wheels have independent rubber suspension so you get the silkiest possible ride. And because this is rubber suspension no passenger space is sacrificed. Front-wheel drive saves weight and takes you round corners like a sports car.'

BMC proclaimed the new car to be 'wizardry on wheels' and added that 'posterity will regard August 26th 1959 as a landmark in the development of the popular motor car.'

Female buyers were deliberately targeted, with emphasis being placed on the car's suitability for shopping due to its interior space and parkability. 'Women of the world rejoice,' trilled a typical Austin Seven press release. 'In a man's world a car has been designed with women in mind.'

❖ Cheap and Cheerful ❖

The very first Minis to hit the road were priced at
£496 19s 2d (including purchase tax), cheaper by far
than other small cars in its class. The Austin A40,
launched less than a year before the Mini, cost £639,
the Fiat 600 cost £613, and the rival from Ford, their
1959 105E Anglia, was £589. At £702, the Triumph
Herald couldn't compete on price either. This did
not, however, mean that the Mini was a huge financial
success, quite the contrary. Ford took an early Mini
and dismantled it piece by piece, costing every nut
and bolt, every stage of the production process. Their
verdict was that at £497, in real terms BMC were
losing at least £30 on every car they sold.

❖ Rave Reviews ❖

Following its road test on the new Morris Mini Minor
on August 28, 1959, *Autocar* concluded:

'The Mini is far from being an underpowered
miniature, and has very lively performance;
it is certain to interest the sporting motorist
because of its fine handling. It also scores
in traffic, and its minimum overhang
makes parking an easy matter in cities. The

manufacturers are to be congratulated on producing, at a truly competitive price, an outstanding car providing unusual space for its size, and one in which four persons can enjoy comfortable, safe and economic motoring.'

The Motor was equally enthusiastic and wrote:

'Characteristics which have often been thought utterly incompatible are combined amazingly well in the new 848cc Austin Seven. It is an exceptionally low-priced car which costs little to run, and its overall dimensions are extremely compact. Yet it carries four adults with space to spare, potters with conventional multi-cylinder smoothness or accelerates briskly up to a top speed of well over 70mph, rides comfortably and handles with exceptional precision.'

❖ A Slow Starter ❖

The Mini was slow to take off. The working classes, which were its target market, kept their hands firmly in their pockets. Motorists in general mistrusted it because it was so cheap, and their confidence didn't exactly grow during the first winter – by which time 20,000 had been sold – when a technical fault caused numerous water leaks and rotting carpets, resulting in a number of expensive recalls. Four months after launch, the editor of *Motor Sport* wrote: 'When driving the "World's Most Exciting Car" I found it to live up to its reputation – part of the excitement being to see which foot got wet first!'

Another journalist made his point by inviting a Longbridge press officer to come outside and have a look inside his Mini, where he had installed goldfish swimming around in the door pockets. Competitors cheekily advised customers who were thinking of buying a Mini to ask for the free pair of BMC Wellington boots.

These problems didn't manifest themselves earlier because the Mini was launched in the summer and most of the testing had been done in dry weather. In any case, Issigonis appeared to be in denial about such problems, even after water had seeped up his tweed trousers during a test drive through puddles. Another member of the design team, Barry Kelkin, remembered: 'He [Issigonis] got very irate and shouted, "Stop. Stop. There isn't a problem." Even though the water was actually wicking up his trousers, he just didn't want to believe it.'

Similarly the decision to put the distributor right at the front of the engine, where it was virtually open to the elements, left many a Mini driver stranded whenever it rained, which it did rather a lot in the winter of 1959-60. Eventually a card sheet was fitted to protect against the worst of the rain. Prolonged spells of wet weather were also known to make the Mini's sliding windows stick as the felt-type seals on them swelled up, such tales merely adding to the public's early caution vis-à-vis the perky little newcomer.

A senior BMC executive later confessed that the Mini had 'quivered on the brink of failure'.

∗∷∗ The Goonmobile ∗∷∗

Among the Mini's many celebrity fans during the 1960s were Goon Show stars Peter Sellers and Spike Milligan. Although Sellers' first Minis were fairly standard production models, he soon progressed to radically upgraded cars.

In 1963, with the instruction, 'Anything you boys can think of, you have my full permission to do,' he commissioned the coachbuilding company Hooper to produce a car with padded, reclining front seats in Connolly leather with contrasting piping; matching leather rear seats as well as a leather trim throughout; a polished mahogany dashboard; the latest in transistor radios with an electric aerial and twin speakers; electric windows; deep pile carpets; a full-length sunroof; the petrol filler cap concealed in the boot and a host of other extras which included an exterior 'wickerwork' trim that was painstakingly hand painted. The car starred with him in his 1964 'Pink Panther' movie *A Shot in the Dark*.

In 1965 he gave girlfriend Britt Ekland a customised Radford mini as a birthday present, driving the car out of a giant paper 'birthday cake' as a publicity stunt at the Radford showroom. The car had an opening tailgate, added, in the words of Sellers, 'so that Harry Secombe could come along'.

Spike Milligan owned several, less exotic, Minis and the car made him feel so fervently patriotic that he once made an advertisement for British Leyland, waiving his usual fee.

❖ Fun in a Mini ❖

'I had a Mini because it was fast, economical, and great fun. That was the main thing. We had different engines, and the one we put in at the end was incredibly fast – a lot faster than my Aston Martin.' – Lord Snowdon

❖ By Royal Approval ❖

The car's reputation was greatly enhanced when Alec Issigonis took the Queen for a test drive in a Mini in Windsor Great Park. Lord Snowdon was a big fan of the little car and went on to become a firm friend of Issigonis, who was so delighted by royal patronage that he allowed Snowdon certain perks, such as the opportunity to drive the car that won the 1965 Monte Carlo Rally. Snowdon's own Mini had a special wind-up window fitted on the driver's side but, at Issigonis's insistence, kept the standard production sliding window on the passenger side because it blew Princess Margaret's hair about less.

✣ Baby Wheels ✣

Issigonis wanted the Mini to have the smallest possible wheels. Of its contemporaries, the Austin A35 was fitted with 13-inch wheels as standard, while the Morris Minor's were 14-inch. But Issigonis was looking at something much smaller because he was only too aware that large wheel arches would take up vital space in the car's interior. When he was eventually asked what size the wheels should be, he held his hands out and spread them to the required dimension. The room fell silent in disbelief. Then one of the Dunlop tyre-making team walked over to Issigonis and measured the gap between his outstretched hands: it was just ten inches. The suggestion immediately alarmed Tommy French of Dunlop who told Issigonis: 'It's impossible. You can't, you couldn't accommodate the brakes.' Issigonis knew it could be done, stuck to his guns, and Dunlop duly delivered the 10-inch wheels.

❖ It Will Never Turn ❖

When the Mini was first announced, motoring journalists were extremely sceptical about its potential handling. There had been small cars before, of course, but this one, with its front-wheel drive layout and transverse engine was thought to be a potential disaster. Some said that it would never corner safely. Senior members of the press were eventually given Minis for long-term testing on loan for 12 months, with an option to buy the car at the end of the year. Many of them did just that.

This fleet of press cars were registered together at Oxford and the licence plates all began with the letters GFC, which someone suggested stood for 'Gifts For Correspondents'.

Although offered the extended loan, the colourful John Bolster of *Autosport* – famed for wearing a deerstalker hat during his many TV appearances – was so impressed with the Mini that he immediately bought one. Within six months, he had clocked up 10,000 miles in the UK and France. Apart from the inevitable damp carpet syndrome, which the service department soon put right, he found the car to be mechanically reliable, and wrote: 'Only an idiot or maniac could possibly have an accident. I am so happy that at last patriotism may be combined with enjoyable motoring.'

❖ Mary Quant's Mini ❖

'It was my first car and I was very proud of it. It was black with black leather seats – a handbag on wheels. Flirty, fun and exciting, it went exactly with the miniskirt.' – Mary Quant

❖ Open Boot ❖

An unusual feature of the first Minis was a top-opening boot-lid which could be left open to create extra luggage space. To accommodate this, the number plate was hinged so that it remained vertical even when the boot was open. Although this was an ingenious idea, drivers complained that heavy cases on the open boot-lid adversely affected the car's handling.

In addition to the boot, luggage could be stored under the Mini's rear seats, and BMC even went so far as to design wicker baskets which would fit into that space. However, the baskets were never actually put on sale through dealerships and the gap was never properly filled by private enterprise either.

❖ Built for Speed ❖

Alec Issigonis and John Cooper first met at the 1946 Brighton Speed Trials, where, as keen motor sport enthusiasts, they found their cars matched against each other on the same run. The Cooper 500 beat Issigonis's Lightweight Special but the race formed the start of a friendship which was to prove beneficial to both men.

By the end of 1960, Cooper had become a successful Formula One team owner with two World Championships under his belt, courtesy of the Australian Jack Brabham. Moreover Cooper was not averse to innovation, his trailblazing Grand Prix cars having the engine unconventionally located behind the driver in a manner reminiscent of the German Auto Unions of the 1930s. So there was nothing about the equally revolutionary Mini that was likely to faze him, and as soon as he drove a pre-production model in 1958, he realised that its handling would lend itself to rallying and racing.

Cooper subsequently discussed the idea with Issigonis but the latter was still focused on the Mini as the car for the man – and woman – in the street. By way of a compromise, Issigonis suggested Cooper ask George Harriman if he could build a run of four-seater GTs. After nothing more than a brief meeting, Harriman gave the go-ahead. Cooper recalled later: 'Harriman said that we had to make 1,000 – but we eventually made 150,000!'

Cooper was convinced there was a market for a four-seater that could match the handling and performance of a Lotus Elite. By fitting what was essentially a Formula Junior race engine into a Mini, he produced a 997cc Mini Cooper with 55bhp and a top speed of 85mph.

The Mini Cooper's appearance in 1961 (price £679) cast reflected glory on to the standard Mini and helped cement its success at a time when its future was still hanging in the balance. In 1962 alone Mini Coopers would win an incredible 153 races.

❧ No Great Enthusiasm ❧

When the Mini 850 first arrived at the BMC motor sport department at Abingdon, Oxfordshire, its potential as a competition car was not immediately obvious. In fact, it just sat in the car park for several days with nobody in a hurry to take it for a spin. One lunchtime, MG's chief mechanic Dougie Watts needed to pop into town, and looked around for a suitable car to borrow. He walked over to the Mini but then changed his mind and took an Austin Healey instead. However, he and his colleagues would soon come to appreciate the Mini's virtues.

❖ Star-Studded Gathering ❖

The sporty Mini Cooper was unveiled to the press on July 17, 1961. Among the guests at the pre-launch dinner at London's Kensington Palace Hotel were no fewer than 27 Grand Prix drivers, including Jack Brabham, Bruce McLaren, Graham Hill, Stirling Moss, John Surtees, Innes Ireland, Phil Hill, Dan Gurney, Wolfgang von Trips, Jo Bonnier, Roy Salvadori and Mike Parkes.

The new car received almost unanimous acclaim. *Motor* magazine summed up its appeal: 'So much performance combined with a lot of practical merit and quite a high standard of refinement will obviously make people decide that a sum of about £600 is better spent on this model than on something bigger but no better.'

Joy was by no means confined to these shores and when *Sports Car Graphic* got hold of the first Mini Cooper to arrive in California, they 'found it difficult to drive without grinning from ear to ear. The performance is so startling for the overall size and appearance that it is ridiculous.'

❖ 'So Damned Ugly' ❖

John Cooper persuaded Alec Issigonis to lend him an early Mini to take to the Italian Grand Prix at Monza in September 1959. Cooper and one of his Formula One drivers, Roy Salvadori, drove there from London and were delighted to find that they had completed the journey quicker than rival team manager Reg Parnell in his Aston Martin.

At Monza, Cooper was spotted driving the Mini around the paddock by Fiat Chief Engineer, Aurelio Lampredi, who begged him for a drive. Lampredi was gone for so long that Cooper became concerned that he had crashed, leaving him with some explaining to do to BMC, but to Cooper's relief, the Italian finally reappeared. On jumping out of the Mini, he said excitedly: 'John, this is the car of the future. If it wasn't so damned ugly, I'd shoot myself!'

❖ Disc Brakes ❖

One of the great advantages of the Mini Cooper was its braking system. Lockheed rose to the challenge of putting disc brakes on those tiny wheels, thereby creating a safer car on ordinary roads as well as allowing for much later braking in competition. Another plus was the John Cooper-designed remote control gear shift to replace the old thin, willowy wand that acted as a gear lever on standard Minis and which was so unstable that drivers were known to fit a length of garden hose over it to provide extra rigidity.

⁘ Not the American Way ⁘

'The principle was to come up with the bare basics for a car, without ostentation, whilst maximising the space available, and making it as fuel-efficient as possible. One of Issigonis's peeves about American cars was the thickness of their doors. He used to say that you could build a whole car out of the metal they used for one door. He was very insistent that the Mini should have thinner, and therefore lighter, doors.' – John Cutler, member of the Mini design team

⁘ Minis by the Million ⁘

In February 1965 the millionth Mini rolled off the production line, ready for delivery to Mr and Mrs Peter James, from Cheshire. It was only the second British car in history to achieve such a momentous production run, the first having been the Morris Minor in 1961.

In June 1969, Sir Alec Issigonis as he had just become, was on hand to celebrate the completion of the two millionth Mini – the first British car to reach that landmark – while the three millionth car had the final trim attached in October 1972.

The Mini passed the four million mark in 1976 and ten years later TV personality Noel Edmonds drove the five millionth car off the Longbridge assembly line.

In April 2007, the twenty-first-century BMW MINI achieved its first million at the company's Cowley plant near Oxford.

⁘ The Wheels Are Off! ⁘

Demonstrably one of the most successful competition cars of all time, the Mini won its first official race shortly after its launch in 1959. With saloon car racer 'Doc' Shepherd at the wheel, the Mini came top of its racing class at Snetterton, with many more glorious sporting achievements to follow.

Racing a Mini was not, however, without its problems, it being particularly difficult to keep up with the racing pack when your wheels have dropped off. Under the extreme pressure of competition, the centres of the Mini's original steel wheels had a tendency to pull out. In the Mini's first Six-Hour

Relay Race at Silverstone, where the corners are long, fast and put huge stress on tyres and wheels, the competing Minis lost so many front wheels that the team had to be withdrawn from the competition. The motorsport authorities eventually banned Minis with the early steel wheels.

⁘ Assembly Line ⁘

In 1959, the Longbridge assembly line was 220 yards (200 metres) long. There were 57 work stations on the line and each task took 2min 24sec, making a little over two hours per car. By the following year, 400 Minis a day were being produced at the Birmingham plant.

⁘ Strictly for the Girls ⁘

With its ability to weave easily in and out of traffic and to fit into an 11ft 6in (3.5m) parking space, it's no wonder the Mini quickly became popular with women drivers. Sixties celebrities such as Twiggy, Mary Quant, Marianne Faithfull, Hayley Mills, Jean Shrimpton, Cathy McGowan, Brigitte Bardot, Princess Alexandra, Lulu, Christine Keeler, Jenny Agutter, Shirley Bassey and Dame Margot Fonteyn all owned Minis.

On August 1, 1967, Marianne Faithfull arrived at the law courts in her two-tone Mini to hear boyfriend Mick Jagger's appeal against his drug sentence. Meanwhile Princess Grace of Monaco regularly drove a Mini around the Principality, and by 1978 half of all Mini buyers were women. More recently Goldie Hawn and Madonna have both owned and loved Minis.

On her 2003 track 'American Life', Madonna utters the immortal line: 'I drive my Mini Cooper and I'm feeling super dooper.'

Don't knock it: it rhymes.

☸ The Flying Sofa ☸

Using a 1300cc Mini engine and assorted Mini parts, Britons Edd China and David Davenport built a sofa that could do nearly 90mph. Making its bow in 1998, the Casual Lofa was a 65bhp leopard skin-upholstered couch that seated three, did 0-60 in 22 seconds and, with an impressive top speed of 87mph, unsurprisingly broke the Guinness World Record for 'Fastest Furniture'. Although the steering wheel was made out of a medium-sized pizza pan and the brake pedal was a cola can, the motorised sofa passed its MOT and was fully roadworthy.

❖ Mini Timeline ❖

1906:   Alec Issigonis born in Smyrna.

1936:   Issigonis joins Morris at Cowley under the
         leadership of Leonard Lord.

1948:   After five years of work, Issigonis's Morris
         Minor is launched.

1952:   The British Motor Corporation (BMC)
         formed by the merger of Austin and Morris.

1955:   Following a few years at Alvis, Issigonis
         teams up with Lord again at BMC.

1957:   Pursuing Lord's demand for a new small
         car, Issigonis and his team create a prototype
         Mini.

1958:   Lord gives the go-ahead for the Mini to
         enter production.

1959:   The Mini is launched.

1960:   The Mini Van and estate cars (Traveller and
         Countryman) are added to the range.

1961:   The Mini Cooper is introduced.

1962:   Pat Moss wins the Tulip Rally.

1964:   The Mini wins its first Monte Carlo Rally.

Birth of the Mini Moke.

Hydrolastic suspension replaces rubber on the Mini.

1965:   The one millionth Mini rolls off the production line.

1967:   Mk II Mini is launched at the London Motor Show. It has a wider rear window, new light clusters, bigger grille, and other changes.

First Mini Festival is held at Brands Hatch.

1968:   British Leyland is formed by the merger of BMC and Standard-Triumph.

The cable pull system for opening the Mini's doors is replaced by conventional handles.

1969:   The two millionth Mini is produced.

Minis are the real stars of *The Italian Job*.

The Mini Clubman is launched.

The Mk III Mini has wind-up windows.

The Austin and Morris prefixes are dropped, and the car is known from then on simply as the Mini.

Issigonis is knighted.

1970:   In BL's final full works entry, Paddy Hopkirk drives a Mini Cooper 1275 to second place in the Scottish Rally.

1971: Leyland decides against renewing the Cooper contract.

Issigonis retires from BL.

Rubber suspension reappears on the Mini and stays for the rest of the car's life.

1972: The three millionth Mini is produced.

1976: Mini production passes the four million mark.

1977: Reversing lights, reclining seats, and dipping rear view mirror all become standard across the range.

1979: BL makes a development plan, which includes the proposed axing of the Mini in 1982.

1980: The Austin Mini Metro is launched, using Mini subframes in a hatchback body.

The unloved Clubman is scrapped, but the classic Mini survives as BL reconsiders its development plan.

1981: The Mini makes its last appearance in the top ten of Britain's best selling cars.

Austin Rover formed as a subsidiary of British Leyland.

1984: All Minis get 12-inch wheels and front disc brakes as standard.

1986: The five millionth Mini is driven off the production line.

1987: Austin Rover becomes just Rover.

1988: Death of Sir Alec Issigonis.

1990: The Mini Cooper returns as a limited edition of 1,650 cars.

1991: The Lamm Cabriolet LE is the first official Mini with 13-inch wheels. Only 75 are produced.

1992: The British Open Classic Mini is the first production Mini with an electric folding sunroof.

1993: The Cabriolet is re-introduced with a Cooper engine and 12-inch wheels.

1994: BMW takes control of the Rover Group.

2000: The last classic Mini leaves the production line at Longbridge.

John Cooper dies on Christmas Eve.

❖ Long-Distance Runner ❖

Although many people perceived the Mini to be a car for making short journeys around town, *Autosport*'s Gregor Grant quickly set out to prove that it could cope with long-distance journeys, too.

Grant took his wife and three children – aged 16, 14 and nine – to Scotland, complete with a sizeable amount of luggage, much of it packed on to a Portarack roof rack. He clocked up 1,000 miles, averaged 44mpg, and the Mini used no oil or water. He calculated that return rail fares would have cost in excess of £22, whereas the petrol for the 810 miles from London to Glasgow and back was less than £4.

❖ A Very Special Cooper ❖

The success of the 997cc Mini Cooper encouraged John Cooper to aim even higher, and in March 1963, the Mini Cooper S was launched with 1071cc to comply with the 1100cc racing class. George Harriman had wanted to call the car the Mini Cooper Special, but eventually decided on just the initial 'S'. With increased power, a stronger gearbox, wider wheels and improved brakes, the Mini Cooper S boasted 70bhp, a top speed of almost 95mph, and a 0-60mph time of less than 13 seconds – half that of the standard Mini.

The Mini Cooper S also compared favourably to BMC's 'proper' sports car with the same A-Series engine, the 1098cc Austin Healey Sprite MkII. This only had 55bhp, and despite having a bigger engine, just two seats and a sleeker shape than the Mini, it could manage just 88mph and took 18 long seconds to get from 0-60mph.

Never one for resting on his laurels, Cooper then wanted to build a car to compete in the 1300cc racing class, and so in 1964 a 1275cc Mini Cooper S was introduced. When Cooper first mooted the idea at a BMC board meeting, Harriman was not sure whether it was possible to get 1275cc out of the existing block. But as Cooper was leaving, Harriman put his arm around him and said: 'We're bloody well going to do it, though!' And they did, producing a flyer that had a top speed of over 97mph and could do 0-60mph in a shade over 11 seconds.

❈ The Mini Down Under ❈

The Mini first went on sale in Australia in March 1961 as the Morris 850 (in recognition of its engine capacity) because the word 'Mini' was thought to have connotations of 'tiny' and 'cheap'. Treating the new car like a baby, Australian newspapers of March 23 that year carried blank page advertisements with a small birth notice in the middle, announcing the arrival of the little Morris. The car was available only in red, white, blue or yellow and BMC thought they would be lucky to sell 10,000. They were quite unprepared for the avalanche of orders that were placed on the first day, and by 1963 the Mini was the third best selling car in Australia, with over 20,000 happy owners. In total, some 212,000 Minis in all guises were sold in Australia.

⁖ Up Periscopes! ⁖

To derive the maximum benefit from its compact dimensions, the Mini needed to have a tight turning circle (32ft/9.75m). There were no existing driveshafts up to the task, so Issigonis had to adapt the design for a constant velocity joint (invented by a Czech, Hans Rzeppa, in 1926) that had previously been used on submarine periscopes.

⁖ A Friendly Warning ⁖

To mark the production of the two millionth Mini in 1969, British Leyland (which had been formed from the merger of BMC and Standard-Triumph) issued a rear window sticker for Minis saying, 'Don't play rough – I've got two million friends.'

❈ Dream Machine ❈

'For thousands of us who had to get around London quickly, the arrival of the Mini was like the answer to a prayer.' – Peter Sellers

❈ Longbridge Car Park ❈

Although labour and supply problems meant that neither Longbridge nor Cowley ran close to its design capacity for long, at any one time when production was at its peak in the 1960s, there could be upward of 10,000 vehicles being finished at Longbridge and over 6,000 at Cowley. Keen to avoid the factories being clogged up with completed but undelivered cars, BMC built a large multi-storey car park at Longbridge. This was just enough to house a few days' production, in case there were any delays in delivery.

❈ Duster's Last Stand ❈

An early reliability problem with the Mini was traced to the fact that one of the plant's cleaning ladies was using a red duster, the hairs from which clogged the carburettors as the cars came off the production line.

❖ Clarkson in a Pickle ❖

'The lovely thing about the Mini is when one goes by, you have no idea what sort of person is at the wheel. It is hard to think of any product that is quite so classless. Branston Pickle maybe, but that's about it.' – Jeremy Clarkson

❖ Flying the Flag ❖

As a show of patriotism in the 1960s, the *Daily Express* thought it would be a great idea to take an aerial photograph of hundreds of red, white and blue Minis in the formation of a Union Jack. The task of putting the plan into practice fell to Cowley PR man Tony Dawson. He borrowed 1,000 Corgi models and worked out a precise layout in miniature before the stunt itself was arranged on waste ground near the plant. A total of 804 Minis was ultimately used to create the flag.

❖ The Car of the Stars ❖

What does George Best have in common with King Hussein of Jordan? Or Clint Eastwood with Charles Aznavour? Or Mick Jagger with Jeffrey Archer? Or even Norman Wisdom with the Aga

Khan? Well, along with the likes of Cliff Richard, Tom Hanks, Eddie Izzard, Peter Cook, King Constantine of Greece, Noel Gallagher, Eddie Van Halen and Prince Michael of Kent, they all owned Minis – as unfortunately did glam rocker Marc Bolan's girlfriend, Gloria Jones. For after enjoying dinner together on the night of September 16, 1977, she drove Bolan home in her purple Mini Cooper 1275 GT (FOX 661L) but shortly after 4am, the car smashed into a tree on the south side of Barnes Common in south-west London, killing Bolan instantly.

❖ Bursting with Pride ❖

'Don't expect me to be modest about the Mini. I'm very proud that it has run for so many years without a major mechanical change and it still looks like the car we designed. Five million people have bought my Mini and it just goes to show that they have a lot of common sense.' – Sir Alec Issigonis in 1986, as sales of the Mini pass five million

❖ Spinning Rod ❖

During the painting of the Mini's shell, a rod was inserted straight through the car, thereby allowing the shell to be rotated so that both the top and bottom of the vehicle could be painted easily. The speedometer dial, which with its fuel gauge insert made up the entire instrument panel on early models, was originally put in the middle of the dashboard to cover the hole where the pole went.

⁖ The Lap of Luxury ⁖

From 1963, distinguished coachbuilder Harold Radford created Minis with luxury interiors under the label of the Mini de Ville. He was no stranger to such work. At the 1957 Motor Show at Earl's Court, he exhibited a Bentley Countryman that had a pull-out picnic table, a warm-water washbasin and an espresso machine in the rear.

By 1967 the Radford Mini de Ville MkIII cost £3,000 more than a basic Mini, but it came complete with a dazzling array of extras: sun roof, twin speakers, electric windows, automatic reversing light, electric screen washers, hazard flashers, seat belts, and self-parking wipers. That year, Mike Nesmith of the Monkees paid £3,640 for a Radford Mini, making it the most expensive Mini that had yet been built. Designed to his own specifications, it included a 1275 S engine, given extra bite by renowned Mini tuners Downton, a radio and tape system, special ventilation to cope with the California climate, and 'pink champagne' upholstery.

Another firm which specialised in creating luxurious Minis was Wood & Pickett. Bill Wood and Les Pickett left their jobs at London coachbuilder's Hooper & Co in 1947 to start their own business, in the early days operating from Wood's living room. Inspired by the success of Radford's Mini de Ville, Wood & Pickett developed their own upmarket Mini, known as the Margrave, which featured a distinctive leather and walnut fascia panel, leather or Dralon seating and a list of individually-priced optional extras.

Flamboyant actor Laurence Harvey spent £3,500 on a 1970 Wood & Pickett Mini Cooper S, which had darkened windows, a full-size sunroof, soft wool carpets and linings, Connolly leather on the seats, doors and dashboard, electric windows, a superb in-car entertainment system and, as a finishing touch, his own initials in gold on the doors.

Not to be outdone, by the late 1970s wealthy Arabs were paying up to £20,000 for a Mini containing such essentials as a television, telephone, air-conditioning, electric sun roof and quadraphonic hi-fi system.

❧ Nuts and Bolts ❧

There are a total of 3,016 screws, nuts and bolts on a Mini.

❧ Showdown in the Showroom ❧

'So many people said to me, "You'll never sell that."
They laughed out loud. Not for long though, we could
not get enough of them, some people almost came to
blows in the showroom when it came to allocating
the first Minis.' – UK car salesman Bill Preston

❧ Monte Carlo Marvel ❧

As the Mini's standing as a successful motor-cross and
circuit racer steadily grew, so too did its reputation
as a rally car and giant killer. Irish rally ace Paddy
Hopkirk campaigned a 1275cc Mini Cooper S in the
prestigious Monte Carlo Rally in 1964. A British car's
most recent best performance in the event had been
when a Jaguar Mark VII won in 1956. Otherwise, the
top three places on the winner's rostrum over the years
had been dominated by Mercedes, Porsche, Renault,
Citroën, Lancia and Saab.

Despite nearly being arrested for driving the
wrong way down a one-way street in France, Hopkirk
won the event outright, with Timo Makinen taking
a Cooper S to first place the following year, too.
Makinen also crossed the line first in 1966, with
Rauno Aaltonen's Mini second and Paddy Hopkirk's
coming third. However, a Mini hat-trick was too

much for the French organisers to bear, and afterwards, determined to find an irregularity, they subjected the three cars to eight hours of intense inspection. Eventually they concluded that the dipped pattern of the Minis' headlamps did not conform to the rules, and all three were disqualified, conveniently allowing a Citroën to take first place. The winning driver, Pauli Toivonen, was so embarrassed at what he called a 'hollow victory' that he boycotted the post-rally awards ceremony and vowed never to drive for Citroën again.

Undaunted, Aaltonen was back in 1967, taking his Mini Cooper S to first place again, with Lancia second and Porsche third. This time there was no dispute, although it was the last time the plucky little British Mini would deny the mighty warriors of the rallying world a win in Monte Carlo.

That was largely because when British Leyland came into force under Lord Stokes in 1968, one of the first decisions made by the new management was that Minis should compete on the track rather than in rallies, because circuit racing was much cheaper. Rallying was to continue in a reduced fashion, but only in countries where it was thought to have a direct benefit on sales. The all-conquering rally team was disbanded and the Abingdon competitions department was closed down completely in 1970.

❖ Nudge Bars ❖

To protect their Mini's bumper in busy city traffic, many owners invested in the Mini nudge bar, available through BMC dealers for 99s 6d – that's just under £5 in Sixties money.

❖ The Lowest Mini ❖

In 1985, Dorset custom car enthusiast Andy Saunders chopped over 17 inches (43cm) off the height of a standard Mini estate that he had bought for £10 to create what was then the world's lowest car. The 34½-inch (87cm) high purple mini Mini, named 'Claustrophobia', was even road-legal. The only thing he couldn't lower on it was the engine, so he cut a hole in the bonnet and left the engine protruding through the top. He took out the original seats and replaced them with white vinyl garden chairs, their legs removed and the chairs set in a reclining position. Incidentally, Saunders has recently modified a Fiat to a height of just 21 inches (53cm).

Two years earlier, Saunders had built another abridged Mini, the 1300cc Mini Ha Ha. Here he cut a standard Mini into three pieces and shortened it by 2ft 7in (79cm), taking out the front seats and surrounding cabin section. The driver sat in the same place relative to the steering wheel and pedals as before, but this time was sitting on the rear seat. The result of 750 hours' work, the tiny car could actually do wheelies in reverse gear! Saunders was so pleased with his work that he went on to build two more Mini Ha Has.

❖ The De Luxe Version ❖

Priced at £40 more than the basic Mini in 1959, the De Luxe version had carpets instead of rubber mats, an adjustable seat on the passenger side, opening rear side windows, bumper overriders, an extra sun visor on the passenger side, two-tone vinyl upholstery, foam seat cushions, full width wheel trims and a heater. Although BMC had thought that a four-seater car for under £500 would be a great selling point, most Mini buyers were happy to pay the extra money to acquire the De Luxe version instead – another indicator perhaps that the company had priced the car unnecessarily cheaply.

❖ Pulling Power ❖

'The Mini was viewed by women as part of the family, as something for running the kids around and for shopping. But for many guys it was a little hot rod for attracting the chicks and racing up the road in.' – Artist Alan Aldridge

❖ Best Seller ❖

Although it is always viewed as a Sixties icon, the Mini's peak production year was 1971 when 318,475 cars were sold worldwide. Here are the Mini's worldwide production figures year by year:

1959:	19,749	**1980:**	150,067
1960:	116,677	**1981:**	69,986
1961:	157,059	**1982:**	56,297
1962:	216,087	**1983:**	49,956
1963:	236,713	**1984:**	35,038
1964:	244,359	**1985:**	34,974
1965:	221,974	**1986:**	33,720
1966:	213,694	**1987:**	37,210
1967:	237,227	**1988:**	36,574
1968:	246,066	**1989:**	40,998
1969:	254,957	**1990:**	46,045
1970:	278,950	**1991:**	35,007
1971:	318,475	**1992:**	26,197
1972:	306,937	**1993:**	20,468
1973:	295,186	**1994:**	20,417
1974:	255,336	**1995:**	20,378
1975:	200,293	**1996:**	15,638
1976:	203,575	**1997:**	16,928
1977:	214,134	**1998:**	14,311
1978:	196,799	**1999:**	11,378
1979:	165,502	**2000:**	7,070

❖ Like Driving a Go-Kart ❖

The Mini's first suspension system, designed by Issigonis's friend Dr Alex Moulton (inventor of the Moulton bicycle), used compact rubber cones rather than conventional springs. This ingenious design reduced the overall size of the suspension, meaning that it took up less room in a car where space was at a premium. The use of rubber cones resulted in a somewhat bumpy ride but their rigidity, allied to the fact that the wheels were pushed out to the very corners of the car, led many drivers to enthuse that the Mini handled like a go-kart.

In 1964, the suspension in the upper-range models was replaced by a Hydrolastic system. This new suspension created a softer ride, but it also increased weight and production cost, and in the minds of many enthusiasts, marred the adventurous handling for which the Mini had become famous. So in 1971 the original rubber suspension returned and stayed for the rest of the Mini's life.

❖ Advantage – Mini ❖

Introduced in 1987, the limited edition Mini Advantage was meant to be called the Mini Wimbledon, but the All England Lawn Tennis Club objected to the name. Nevertheless the car retained its tennis theme and was launched to coincide with the start of that year's French Open tournament. The car had full-length tennis netting graphics running between the front and rear wheel arches, with 'Advantage' logos featuring on the doors and the top right of the boot lid.

❖ Your Starter For Ten ❖

Issigonis was determined to keep the Mini light – at 1,380lb it would weigh in excess of 100lb less than the old Austin A35 – and to this end, he mounted the start button on the floor close to the driver's heels, where it was right next to the heavy-duty cable that led from the engine to the boot-housed battery. To have mounted it further forward would have required extra refinements, thereby increasing the car's weight. Indeed it was some years before the floor button on the Mini was replaced by the more familiar key starter.

BMC engineer Dennis Harold recalled: 'For the floor-mounted starter switch Issigonis tried to insist that I had a bare aluminium rod along the bottom of the car from the battery to the switch. I said: "But it is live from the battery. If a mechanic gets a spanner across it, there will be a firework display." We had one or two little upsets with him like that.'

❧ A Cut Above ❧

In 2006, the owner of a hairdressing salon in Beverley, Yorkshire, installed the front end of a classic Mini Cooper as a reception desk. The converted vehicle has the number plate SALON 55 and working lights and indicators. Salon owner Keeley Penn says: 'When I saw it for sale, I just could not resist it. It has the till behind it so it is practical and all the customers love it.'

❧ Mini Bus? ❧

BMC were delighted when some police forces in the UK adopted the Mini as a patrol car, proudly displaying that fact that four hulking great coppers could easily fit inside a standard Mini. There's room for far more than four in a Mini, though! In 2006, 21 students from a Kuala Lumpur college stuffed themselves into a 1999 lime green Mini Cooper in a total of four minutes. They waited the 20 seconds that it would take for them to make it into the Guinness Book of World Records and also claimed that they met the Guinness Book of World Records requirements that said those involved must be over 4ft 11in (1.5m) tall. The previous record was set by 18 women in 2000.

❖ Travelling in Style ❖

Hollywood star Kevin Spacey, who has a dog named Mini, rented a Mini-Limo for his thirty-ninth birthday and had himself chauffered around London in it.

❖ A Work of Art ❖

Motoring aficionados across the globe have long hailed the Mini as a work of art, but Texan Scott Wade has taken the link a step further. He drives his Mini Cooper up and down a one-and-a-half-mile dirt road near his home in San Marcos and then recreates great works of art in the dust on the rear windscreen. By using his fingers, ice lolly sticks and paintbrushes, he has adorned his Mini with dust copies of such famous paintings as the 'Mona Lisa' and Van Gogh's 'Starry Night'. Of course his class is purely temporary – a shower of rain simply washes it away.

❖ The Early Bird... ❖

Although the Mini was by no means an instant success, as the first small car on the market it swallowed up the lion's share of the sales. The Hillman Imp did not

appear until three years later – which cost its owners
Rootes an estimated £9 million in lost sales.

·⁘· Quick Around the Corners ·⁘·

When Dunlop was developing the special tyres
needed for the Mini's tiny wheels, it tested the car's
cornering ability at speed on a wet test track. The
Mini clocked an impressive 44 mph, second only to
the Aston Martin DB4's 46mph. In comparison, the
Morris Minor managed 42mph while the Citroën's
best was a meagre 33mph and the Renault Dauphine
tipped over before it even reached that speed. This
ability to corner at speed encouraged owners to start
racing their Minis.

In its very first road test of the Mini in August
1959, *Autocar* praised the car's handling at speed. It
wrote:

'The all-new suspension has brought about a high
level of stability and road-holding. Steering is light
and accurate.... When fast cornering is indulged
in, the behaviour is predictable and the car plays no
tricks; wet or dry, one never feels any doubt that the
car will get around.'

As a word of warning, it did add: 'However,
oversteer can be produced by too-fast cornering with
a full complement of passengers and a loaded boot.'

❖ Belt Up! ❖

The original Mini was a very basic car and built to the designer's personal taste. Issigonis didn't like car radios or seat belts, so he didn't build them into the Mini, but because he was a chain-smoker, he included an ashtray. When seat belts were later added, they presented a problem for drivers who found it was difficult – sometimes impossible – to reach the gear lever while wearing a properly fastened seat belt.

To make the car shorter, Issigonis had pushed the seats as far forward as possible and had set the driving seat in a more upright position than was usual. The Mini's uncomfortable seats drove many an owner to distraction, while the low roof meant that tall people were forced to become contortionists. Yet it was all apparently a deliberate ploy on the part of the designer, for Issigonis reasoned that the driver should never be too comfortable in case he or she lost concentration at the wheel. In a Mini, there was rarely much chance of that happening.

❖ The Mini Gets a Makeover ❖

In 1967 the Mini received its first facelift in eight years with the introduction of the Mark II. For the first time the 998cc engine became available in the standard Mini shell (albeit in the Super De Luxe version) and the car's turning circle was reduced from 32ft (9.75m) to 28ft (8.5m). The rear window was enlarged, the flashing indicator warning light was moved to the speedometer, and the windscreen wipers automatically parked themselves once they were switched off.

In spite of these improvements, it was pretty much business as usual, with BMC sticking to the maxim: 'If it ain't broke, don't fix it.' This prompted some motoring journals to express regret that a more radical overhaul had not taken place. *Autocar* wrote:

'We were expecting the new Mini to be announced with winding windows, like certain versions built in Australia. This must now be the only car without them, and they are sadly missed. It is also time such economies as cable release interior door handles were brought up to date; and some of the standards of fit and finish were disappointing. Carpets still do not lie snugly on the floor – a criticism we made in 1959.'

Nevertheless the magazine admitted that the Mini was still 'a tremendously practical and dynamic little car that has few equals for town use, or as the second family transport.'

❖ Artistic Mini ❖

For a 1965 commission for the *Sunday Times*, British artist Alan Aldridge whitewashed a hired Mini before decorating it with over 100 tubes of gouache and six cans of silver spray paint. The result depicted a psychedelic car with a split personality – driven by two opposing characters, a boy racer and a housewife. Aldridge had just two days to paint the car before it was photographed and he then spent hours washing off his hard work prior to the Mini's return to the hire company. Shortly afterwards he received an offer of £800 for it from an art collector – more than twice what the unpainted car was worth – but he had to turn it down as the artwork no longer existed.

❖ Maximum Publicity ❖

BMC understandably sought to capitalise on Paddy Hopkirk's epic 1964 Monte Carlo Rally win, realising that the wave of publicity would have a beneficial effect on sales of the ordinary road Mini Cooper S. Beneath a photo of Hopkirk's winning car tackling a mountain hairpin, newspaper and magazine adverts proclaimed: 'Your BMC car may never have to take the pounding of an international rally (but it's nice to know that it could).'

❖ A Car for All Seasons ❖

Hot on the heels of the original Mini came a range of adaptations designed to show that there was a Mini for every occasion. In June 1960, the Minivan was launched at £360, then in September of that same year windows were installed in the van's bodywork to create an estate car, the Austin Seven Countryman or Morris Mini Traveller, the more upmarket versions of which even had wood trim similar to that fitted to the Morris Minor Traveller.

To create the 'Woody' – as it became known – the strips of wood were simply glued to the flanks and rear doors of the Mini. Visible timberwork was seen as adding to the car's class but apparently Issigonis was appalled by such snobbery and considered the whole affair rather tacky.

With its four-inch (10cm) longer wheelbase and overall increase in length of 10 inches (25cm), the Mini estate (price £623) could carry even more by way of luggage and was seen as ideal for family picnics, the hampers being loaded via double 'barn door'-style rear doors.

Then in February 1961, the Mini pickup appeared, identical to the van except for the missing rear section roof and side panels.

❖ A Private Man ❖

'I am often told that I ought to be glad to be known as the man who made the Mini. Well, let me tell you that I don't really enjoy it. I am proud of the Mini, yes, but the whole business of becoming well known because of a car is much more harrowing than the man-in-the-street – or the car – would imagine.' – Alec Issigonis, 1964

❖ The Mini with a Big Engine ❖

The original Mini engine was only 848cc and produced about 34bhp, but one of the largest engines ever installed in the car was a 3.5 litre Buick V8 rated at 220bhp. The car was built in 1964 and was still front-wheel drive, although the engine was actually in the back!

❖ A Mobile Off-Licence ❖

Since the Mini's doors incorporated sliding windows, there was space for deep storage pockets to be installed where a winding window mechanism would normally have been. Issigonis joked that he had designed these pockets to be large enough to contain the ingredients, in precise proportion, of his favourite drink, a dry

Martini, which in his view required 27 bottles of gin to one of dry vermouth. An early press photograph took up the theme, showing a Mini front door pocket crammed with nine gin bottles, and with room for one more.

❖ The Wizard in the Blizzard ❖

Timo Makinen's victory in the 1965 Monte Carlo Rally was achieved in appalling weather conditions, even by the standards of the French Alps in January. Defying the snow and ice, he was the only driver in the field to complete the entire rally without incurring a single penalty point. So bad was the weather en route that only 35 out of 237 starters reached the finish – and three of them were Minis.

❖ Historic Car ❖

Built at Longbridge on November 26, 1964, Austin Mini Cooper S DJB 93B won the 1965 RAC Rally for Rauno Aaltonen and the 1966 Scottish Rally for Tony Fall. It was retired after an accident in the 1966 Gulf London Rally and not rediscovered until 1986. Thereafter it became successful in hill climbs, winning the 2001 Midland Speed Classic Championship. The restored car was sold to a UK private collector for £100,500 at the Bonhams Race Retro auction at Stoneleigh in 2007.

❖ Miles Better ❖

Although the advertising at the launch of the Mini promised an enticing 50 miles per gallon, in the event 40mpg became a more realistic figure. Nevertheless this compared favourably to its rivals in 1959. The Ford Anglia 105E did 36mpg, the Volkswagen Beetle did 34mpg, and the Triumph Herald did 32mpg, while the Ford Popular 100E could only manage 30mpg.

❖ Fine Tuning ❖

In the 1960s, the name of Downton was every bit as synonymous with Minis as Radford, Wood & Pickett and Paddy Hopkirk. Anyone with money to spare and who was looking for that extra bit of performance from their Mini would have the engine tuned by the Downton Engineering Works. A 1275 Mini Cooper S with Downton tuning was just about the hottest drive in town.

The firm that would eventually play a major part in transforming the world of rallying sprang up from a small rural Wiltshire garage, situated in the village of

Downton, south of Salisbury. In 1947, the garage was bought by Daniel Richmond and his wife Veronica, known to her friends as Bunty. Daniel later claimed that he had really only bought the place for the excellent local salmon fishing. Before long, however, the Richmonds developed a reputation for servicing and tuning vintage cars, and it was not uncommon to see Rolls-Royces, Bugattis and Lagondas sharing the forecourt with Morris Minors and Ford Populars.

In the late 1950s the decision was taken to specialise in BMC cars, although it is possible that the change in emphasis did not meet with the immediate approval of the formidable Bunty, who enjoyed the prestige associated with a better class of car. On one occasion she was said to have told a mechanic working on a BMC A-Series engine to take that 'horrible little engine' out of her workshop at once. Since her word was usually law, the rest of the job was finished under a tree in the yard.

The turning point in Downton's fortunes came in December 1961 when *Autocar* published an article headlined 'Mini-Ton-Bomb' about a Downton-converted Mini Cooper that could do 100mph and was easier to drive, quieter, and more fuel efficient than the standard model. Riding on the back of such invaluable publicity, a Downton-modified Mini Cooper competed in the 1962 Targa Florio road race in Italy, where it outperformed many of its bigger rivals. The Richmonds then began supplying BMC with modified engine components for competition cars and even fitted a Downton tuning kit to Alec Issigonis's own Mini. BMC was so impressed that Daniel was offered work as a design consultant, the fee from which enabled him to buy his first stretch of salmon fishing river. Issigonis regularly placed intolerable demands on Richmond – as he did on anyone who would let him – and Daniel often had to work through the night to have a piece of testing or experimentation ready for Issigonis by the following morning.

Soon everyone who was anyone wanted their Mini to be tuned by Downton, but, regardless of status or fame, Bunty still insisted that all customers paid by cash. When a royal equerry was dispatched to Wiltshire to collect a newly modified car for Lord Snowdon and presented a cheque by way of payment, Mrs Richmond bluntly ordered him to go away and come back with cash. The equerry had to stay overnight in the village and re-present himself the following day once the necessary cash had been wired to him from Buckingham Palace.

By the late 1960s Downton was producing up to 100 tuning kits a week and employing more than 80 people but things fell apart after Daniel, who had always been fond of a drink, died suddenly in 1974. Bunty soldiered on for a while but without much enthusiasm. Then in early 1976, her beloved bull terrier Samantha died. The next morning, the Richmonds' cleaning lady, Mrs Vincent, let herself into the family home and found a note telling her not to go into the bedroom but to call the appropriate services as Mrs Richmond had taken her own life.

Bunty had left instructions that their Mini UHR 850, which Daniel had used on road and track to test and promote their business, should either be given to a museum or destroyed by fire. Fortunately the first option was chosen, and the car now resides at the Heritage Motor Centre in Gaydon, Warwickshire.

❖ Mini Hot Tub ❖

For a college design project, British student Matt Worden paid £180 for an old Mini Cooper and turned it into a stylish hot tub. By fitting the interior with a pond liner, he was able to install a luxury whirlpool bath. He replaced the engine with a barbecue, put a drinks fridge where the exhaust used to be and rounded off his luxurious spa by adding a quality sound system.

❊ Pile In! ❊

An early BMC magazine advertisement for the Morris Mini Traveller extolled the virtues of family outings in the car, claiming that there was room for everything... except the kitchen sink. 'Room for a lively, sprawling family! Room for all their everyday extras! Room for their special holiday luggage – and then room to spare! Open those wide rear doors. In go the golf clubs, the weekend cases and the picnic basket. How about junior's bike? No trouble at all – and by folding the rear seats forward you can have more room still whenever you want it. Round to the front now – everybody in. Plenty of space for Dad's long legs. Mother's skirt won't get crushed or crumpled in this roomy Traveller. And the children – not to mention the puppy – have got real space to spread themselves!'

❊ Car of the Century ❊

In 1995, to mark its one-hundredth anniversary, *Autocar* named the Mini as its car of the century. Then a year later it was named Number One Classic Car of All Time by *Classic & Sports Car* magazine. But in 1999 in Las Vegas, the Mini was beaten into second place by the Model T Ford in a Dutch-organised international contest to decide the most influential car of the twentieth century. Choosing from a list of 27 nominees, jurors from 33 countries awarded the Model T 742 points, ahead of the Mini on 617, followed by the Citroën DS (567), the Volkswagen Beetle (521) and the Porsche 911 (303).

❖ Head Case ❖

In 1999, British strongman John Evans balanced a 352-lb (160kg) Mini on his head for 33 seconds. Don't ask why.

❖ The Road to Conversion ❖

When the Mini was launched, vans were categorised as business equipment and as such were not subject to purchase tax, meaning that, in the case of the two-seater Minivan, a 70mph-plus vehicle could be bought for a mere £360. For many it was a bargain that was too good to miss even though the legal speed limit at the time for vans was only 30mph (40mph on the motorway).

BMC saw an opportunity to cash in and marketed a conversion kit to turn the van into a four-seater for just £15. The downside was that the bargain vehicle still had no rear side windows as putting them in would not only have proved expensive but would also have immediately made it liable for purchase tax. So anybody sitting on the optional back seat had visibility which at best was severely restricted.

❖ Not the First Mini! ❖

BMC's wasn't the first car to carry the name Mini. Since 1949 Sharp's Commercials Ltd of Preston had produced a range of three-wheelers called Bond Minicars. These had a front-mounted Villiers two-stroke motorcycle engine driving the single front wheel by means of a chain. The Minicar was conceived and designed by Lawrie Bond – and in 1964 Sharp's Commercials changed its name to Bond Cars Ltd.

❖ Dealer Caution ❖

Car dealers didn't exactly welcome the Mini at first. Their spares and service departments were frightened by the car's complex set-up, the engine accessibility of the Mini being so awkward in comparison to more conventional cars that garage mechanics would throw up their hands in horror at the sight of a Mini in their service bays. Also it was a cheap car, which resulted in low profit margins, and its early unreliability problems used up a lot of time in warranty paperwork.

Eventually, however, the dealers were crying all the way to the bank as the Mini's selling power gave them a continuing turnover on cars, parts, accessories and servicing.

·:· **The Price of Fame** ·:·

Having heard that Paddy Hopkirk was on the brink of winning the 1963 Tour de France car rally in a Mini Cooper, Alec Issigonis made an instant decision to fly out to Monte Carlo with BMC press officer Tony Dawson. But when they arrived at the airport bank in search of some spending money, the bank clerk, mindful of the restrictions on taking currency abroad at that time, would only let them have £5. However, when he spotted Issigonis's name on the passport, his attitude changed.

'Issigonis?' he queried. 'Are you the man that made my Mini?'

'I had something to do with it,' replied Issigonis with uncharacteristic modesty.

'Well, let's make it £25,' said the clerk with a knowing wink.

❖ Vital Statistics ❖

The specifications of the Mini Mk 1 are as follows:

Production Period: 1959–67

Numbers produced (approx.): Austin 435,500; Morris 510,100

Engine: 848cc

Engine bore and stroke: 62.9 x 68.3mm

Power: 34bhp @ 5500rpm

Torque: 44lb @ 2900rpm

Suspension: Rubber cones until Sept 1964, then Hydrolastic

Brakes: Drums front and rear

Wheelbase: 2036mm (saloon); 2138mm (estate)

Length: 3054mm (saloon); 3299mm (estate)

Width: 1397mm; 1410mm (estate)

Height: 1346mm; 1359mm (estate)

Kerb weight: 626kg; 648kg (estate)

The specifications of the Mini Cooper S Mk 1 are as follows:

Production period: 1964–67

Numbers produced (approx.): Austin 6,489;
  Morris 7,824

Engine: 1275cc

Engine bore and stroke: 70.6 x 81.3mm

Power: 76bhp @ 5800rpm

Torque: 79lb @ 3000rpm

Suspension: Rubber cones until Sept 1964, then
  Hydrolastic

Brakes: Disc front, drum rear

Wheelbase: 2036mm

Length: 3054mm

Width: 1397mm

Height: 1346mm

Kerb weight: 640kg

❖ My First Mini ❖

'My favourite car of all time will always be my first Mini. It was tremendous fun.' – Twiggy

❖ Taking the Roof Off ❖

In 1963, Crayford Engineering, of Westerham, Kent, introduced a convertible Mini. The conversion work cost £150 and the company offered two options – one retaining the rear side windows, the other dispensing with them. In all, Crayford converted around 800 Minis. It was another 28 years before the Mini's owners got round to producing a convertible – in the shape of the Rover Mini Cabriolet.

The first Cabriolets – a total of 75 – were built by one of Rover's German franchises, LAMM Autohaus, and were available only in Cherry Red. They had plastic rear side windows, whereas when Rover introduced its own version two years later in 1993, the windows were wind-down glass – the only Mini to have wind-down rear windows.

❖ The Crayford Clubman Convertible ❖

At a conversion price of £195, Crayford launched the Mini Clubman Cameo Convertible in the early 1970s.

Its promotional material read: 'The Cameo is the latest convertible variant based on the Mini theme. It is the result of many years of development and production by Crayford and utilises the very latest chassis installation to ensure maximum torsional rigidity. The rear windows remain in place in their original form with opening clasp permitting full ventilation as on the original saloon, and the convertible top folds down in one easy action. Standard hood colour is black, but other hood colours are available at a surcharge of £45. The Mini Cameo represents the ideal four-seater convertible as there are no restrictions whatever on the original Mini seating and the car is draughtproof and perfectly tailored to produce an attractive and practical sports convertible.'

⁘ Pleasing to the Eye ⁘

'The Mini is a design classic that has lasted such a long time because it is functional, economical, but above all pleasing to the eye.' – Kate Moss

⁘ The Italian Job ⁘

For many, the Mini's finest hour was in the 1969 crime caper *The Italian Job*, starring Michael Caine (who hadn't passed his driving test at the time of filming) as the leader of a gang of gold bullion thieves. In the memorable car chase sequence, the gang drive three Mk 1 Austin Mini Cooper S cars – one red, one white, one blue in keeping with the patriotic theme – down staircases, through storm drains, over buildings and finally into the back of a moving bus. The 60-ft (20m) rooftop jump was particularly hair-raising and so alarmed the film crew that one Italian cameraman had a nervous breakdown beforehand, ran off the set and wasn't found until several hours later! To achieve the jump, the cars had to hit the ramps at 70mph. They only did one take each, after which they were good for nothing but spares.

Very few modifications were made to the cars for the jaw-dropping stunts, the only real problem for Remy Julienne's team of stunt drivers being that the cars had a low ground clearance. Although only the three cars appeared on screen, some 16 Minis were required to perform the film's stunts. The ones thrown out of the bus were ordinary Minis that were dressed up to look like Coopers.

Incidentally, the licence plate on the red Mini was HMP 729G, the white Mini was GPF 146G, and the blue Mini was LGW 809G. The plates, which later sold for £19,800 at auction, each related to something specific in the film. The first was Charlie Croker (Michael Caine)'s prison number, the second came from the Grand Prix flag, and the third was the gang's flight number. Not a lot of people know that.

❖ Fiat Gatecrash the Party ❖

BMC very nearly blew *The Italian Job*. Failing to grasp the public relations opportunity provided by the film, BMC was less than co-operative, eventually agreeing to sell the production company six Minis at trade price but demanding retail price for the remainder. By contrast, Fiat chairman Gianni Agnelli provided complimentary Fiat Dinos as studio cars and used his influence with the local police to have the traffic in Turin stopped while the chase sequences were filmed. He also very nearly persuaded the producers to replace Minis with Fiats, but fortunately for BMC, scriptwriter Troy Kennedy Martin wouldn't hear of it.

'The idea behind the script,' said Kennedy Martin, 'was a gentle send-up of British chauvinism and the Common Market, with all these criminals coming together and the solid British set against the cunning Europeans. The Minis came through in the film as a powerful symbol of what we can do in Britain; they were the most remarkable elements of the story.'

BMC may have appeared indifferent but Issigonis was hugely proud of the film and hired a cinema at a cost of £10 10s for a private screening.

❖ The Last of the Classics ❖

The final Mini to leave the production line at Longbridge was a red Mini Cooper Sport on October 4, 2000. It carried the number plate 1959–2000, the driver was Technical Support Manager Geoff Powell, who had worked at Longbridge since 1960, and his passenger was Lulu. Fans were so upset by the passing of their favourite car that later that day many took their Minis on funeral processions through towns and villages.

In 41 years, a total of 5,387,862 Minis had been produced. Apparently if you laid all the Minis ever made end to end, they would stretch from London to Sydney.

❖ Dancing Minis ❖

Formed in 1981, the Russ Swift Mini Display Team perform car dance routines, demonstrations of handbrake parking, and donuts – Swift himself has even appeared on *Top Gear* teaching grannies how to do donuts! He specialises in driving Minis on two wheels and this, combined with his other stunts, means he gets a maximum of three miles from a set of tyres. He also holds the world record for parallel parking in the tightest space – in April 1999 at Bruntingthorpe, Leicestershire, he managed to park a Mini in a space only 13 inches (33cm) longer than the length of the car!

❄ Hedging His Bets ❄

In case Alec Issigonis's design for the Mini proved unworkable, Leonard Lord secretly asked ERA (English Racing Automobiles, noted racing car manufacturers of the 1930s and 1940s) to come up with an alternative idea for a small car. David Hodkin and Laurence Pomeroy, the latter being technical editor of *The Motor* and a strident campaigner for more imaginative British car design, drew up plans for a rear-engined car with pneumatic suspension and huge tail fins. However, tooling the Maximin, as it was known, would have been extraordinarily expensive and anyway as soon as Lord sat in the prototype Mini, the ERA version's fate was sealed.

❄ Not for America ❄

The Mini was always going to struggle in the United States, a nation which prides itself on the sheer enormity of everything. Whether it is burgers or busts, Americans always produce the biggest. So the Mini was never likely to gain mass acceptance, not only because most Texans would have struggled to fit even their hat inside a Mini but also because the long journeys that Americans have to make require a much larger, more comfortable mode of transport than the humble little Mini.

Furthermore, stringent safety and emission regulations which the US Department of Transportation introduced in the late 1960s meant that all new Minis entering the country would have had to be redesigned. As this would inevitably have incurred hefty additional costs, the decision was taken to withdraw the Mini completely from the US market after 1968 – and with parts difficult to obtain, it was estimated that there were no more than a few thousand Minis on US roads by the early 1990s. Indeed Minis became so rare that younger Americans, seeing one for the first time, were not sure what it was or where it had come from. Consequently they used to refer to Minis as 'clown cars', unaware that they were actually seeing one of the most recognisable cars in the rest of the world.

❖ A Supreme Challenge ❖

Alec Issigonis once said that designing a small car presented a much greater challenge than designing a large car. 'Mr Royce had nothing to do,' he noted, perhaps tongue-in-cheek.

❖ Saloon Car Champion ❖

Although the Mini Cooper would go on to take most of the sporting plaudits, it was an ordinary 848cc

Austin Mini Seven that provided BMC with its first racing title. The nine-race 1961 British Saloon Car Championship – featuring events at Snetterton (2), Goodwood, Aintree, Crystal Palace, Silverstone (2), Brands Hatch and Oulton Park – ended in victory for John Whitmore's Mini by nine clear points. It is not known whether Whitmore celebrated his success with his favourite party trick – chewing beer glasses!

❖ Backs of Envelopes ❖

Alec Issigonis's brain worked so fast that he sometimes struggled to explain his ideas verbally to his team, and instead he would often scribble down his thoughts on the backs of envelopes, serviettes, menus, or any scrap of paper that came to hand. These rough diagrams were then taken away and redrawn by the designers, who therefore became accustomed to finding the answer to a complicated – seemingly insoluble – engineering problem on the back of an electricity bill. Jack Daniels would later remark of their respective roles: 'Issi's was the inspiration and mine was the perspiration.'

❖ Mr Bean's Mini ❖

When the hapless Mr Bean (played by Rowan Atkinson) debuted on UK TV screens in 1990, he owned an orange 1969 Morris Mini Mk II (RNT 996H) but typically it was destroyed in an off-screen crash at the end of the first episode. Thereafter his car was an applejack green 1977 Mini with a black bonnet (SLW 287R). He sometimes got dressed in it as he drove and in a running gag, he would remove the steering wheel instead of the key when getting out. On one memorable occasion, our hero packed the interior with so much junk that there was no room for the driver. Resourceful as ever, he proceeded to drive the car with an extended broom while sitting in an armchair strapped to the roof! This device worked admirably until the road went steeply downhill, the head of the broom came off and he ended up driving through the open rear doors of a removal van.

At the 2007 London premiere of the feature film *Mr Bean's Holiday*, Atkinson – a noted car enthusiast who has extolled the virtues of Minis in various motoring magazine articles – drove the green and black Mini into Leicester Square and parked it on the red carpet.

Mr Bean's Mini is on display at the Cars of the Stars Museum in Keswick, where it sits proudly alongside *The Saint*'s Volvo, *Magnum PI*'s Ferrari and the Trotters' Reliant Regal Supervan from *Only Fools and Horses*. People have even been known to hire it for weddings…

❖ A Helping Hand ❖

Competing in the 1967 Italian Rally of the Flowers, Paddy Hopkirk was leading the event when a mile from the end of the last competitive stage, his Mini broke a driveshaft coupling and had to be rescued by tractor. Although the time lost had cost him first place, he knew that he was still in with a chance of a top-three finish if he could somehow reach final control in the town of San Remo – 14 miles further down the road. So he secretly – and illegally – enlisted the help of his service crew's big four-litre Austin Princess to give the Mini a shove up any incline and then virtually allow it to freewheel on the downhill sections. To carry out the ruse, the Princess sat right behind the Mini bumper-to-bumper... except when spectators or prying photographers appeared on the horizon, at which point it made itself scarce.

The approach to San Remo was via a long tunnel, the ideal spot for one final clandestine push. With Hopkirk's co-driver Ron Crellin demanding more speed in order to beat the clock at the last control, the Princess accelerated up to 60mph before giving the Mini a mighty shove out of the tunnel and into daylight. Despite having no power through the wheels and hazardous handling, Hopkirk managed to pick his way skilfully through the narrow streets and glide into the control area.

His time enabled him to take second place overall and although the last few miles had been watched by hundreds of people, including rally officials, police officers and journalists, nobody ever suspected any chicanery.

❖ Brothel on Wheels ❖

The Motor Media Company of London received a request from a wealthy client in 2006 to restyle a 2000 Mini Cooper so that it looked like a brothel! Over £60,000 was spent giving the interior an all red trim, including luxurious red leather sofa and seats, with matching crushed velour cushions, curtains and headlining. Naturally the plush Wilton carpet was also red, as were the lambswool rugs, and the general ambience was topped off by subtle mood lighting – red of course. Meanwhile the boot housed a motorised drinks bar. The Mini brothel was apparently a jokey birthday present for the customer's wife... but six months later it was up for sale after the couple's marriage broke up.

❖ Minis in the Garden ❖

Peter McCallum, a Mini enthusiast from Ballycastle, County Antrim, Northern Ireland, holds an annual event called Minis in the Garden, where he squeezes over 40 Minis into his garden.

❉ Colour Coding ❉

The works Mini Cooper rally cars were always painted red with a white roof while their circuit racing counterparts were dark green with white bonnet stripes and a white roof. Naturally these colours were soon much in demand among aspiring boy racers.

❉ A Glamorous Accessory ❉

'The first time that I drove that car was the Tour de France in 1963 where, with the handicap system, we led the damn thing. It was on television in France for about 20 minutes every day and I was beating the big Ford Falcons on all the circuits. The French went mad about it and the French dealers all started ordering more Minis. I think it was the first time that BMC realised the potential of the publicity value of motor sport. After that the car became very fashionable. I mean, it was more impressive to pick your girlfriend up in Paris in a Mini than in an E-type Jag!' – Paddy Hopkirk

❉ Nought to Sixty ❉

When introduced in 1959, the Mini could go from 0-60mph in 26.5 sec, compared to 29.4sec (Ford Anglia 105E), 30.4sec (Triumph Herald), 31.3sec

(Morris Minor 1000), 36.4 sec (Ford Popular 100E) and 43.9sec (Renault Dauphine).

❖ Master of the Handbrake Turn ❖

If ever a car was built for the handbrake turn, it was the Mini... as Rauno Aaltonen demonstrated to a gathering of journalists at a BMC open day in the 1960s. To achieve maximum effect, the tyres of his Mini Cooper were pumped up hard and a stretch of tarmac was heavily watered. Then, with Alec Issigonis as his passenger, Aaltonen flew down the track until the car hit the water, whereupon he spun it neatly through 180 degrees, continuing backwards along the same course for a few yards before again turning the car through 180 degrees and carrying on flat out in the original direction. It was beautifully – almost seamlessly – done and topped only in the journalists' eyes by the sight of Issigonis himself then taking the wheel and repeating the feat.

❖ The First Rally Car ❖

The first works Mini to compete in an international sporting event was YOP 663, driven by BMC team manager Marcus Chambers at the Norwegian Viking Rally in September 1959. It finished 51st overall.

The following April, a Mini driven by Suffolk farming brothers Don and Erle Morley won its class in finishing 14th overall at the Geneva Rally.

❊ Testing, Testing ❊

Since he was designing a car for ordinary people, Alec Issigonis wanted the prototype of the Mini to be test-driven by ordinary people, reasoning that he wouldn't learn as much from expert drivers. He admitted that his ideal tester would be 'my old mother who could break anything'. So he chose two engineers from the Longbridge plant – Bill Appleby and Harry Gardner – and sent them off to the nearby Lickey Hills in a rudimentary version of the XC/9003 prototype with a 948cc engine. They quickly proved his point by rolling the car. When Gardner returned with a cut head, Issigonis is said to have panicked for fear that the new car would end up killing people, and so he decided to use a short-throw crankshaft to reduce the capacity to 848cc.

❊ The Lightweight Special ❊

The 750cc single-seater Lightweight Special, which Alec Issigonis built entirely by hand with his friend George Dowson and raced intermittently in hill climbs and speed trials from 1938, embodied several design innovations that he would later incorporate in the Mini.

As its name implies, the weight was kept to a minimum, the end product tipping the scales at around 1,100lb, partly because, instead of having a conventional chassis, it had side sandwich panels made of plywood covered in aluminium sheet. Unusually for the time, Issigonis used rubber springing in the suspension − another idea that would resurface in the Mini − while the angle of the steering wheel in the two cars was almost identical. Even the method employed to design the cars was similar: rather than use traditional engineering drawings, Issigonis sketched everything true to life before turning these sketches into the finished car.

Issigonis himself played down comparisons, later describing the Lightweight Special as 'a frivolity in my life. It was not so much a design exercise as a means of teaching me to use my hands.' In fact, by the end of the 1940s his bosses at Morris had virtually banned him from racing anyway − but not before his design had proved its worth. Powered by an Austin Seven Ulster engine, the Lightweight Special beat a works Austin with the same engine at the Prescott Hill Climb in 1939.

One other thing the Lightweight Special and the Mini have in common is that both were built to last, and the single-seater still takes part in occasional hill climbs and speed events over 70 years after its creation.

❧ Death of the Sidecar ❧

The Mini was hailed as being single-handedly responsible for the demise of the motorcycle and sidecar. Why should three people have to brave the elements in a bike and sidecar when, for a little more money, four could travel in comfort under the roof of a Mini? Nowhere was the switch more apparent than at the AA where, in 1967, they abandoned the familiar motorcycle combination in favour of a fleet of gleaming new Minivans.

❧ The Word ❧

Leonard Lord used the word 'mini' as early as January 1947 when he told Austin shareholders that he was not yet proposing to make a mini car. This is probably when the term was first used in reference to a small economy vehicle.

❧ Heated Debate ❧

In the original Mini, the radiator was mounted at the left side of the car so that the engine-mounted fan could be retained, but while this arrangement saved precious length, it had the disadvantage of feeding the radiator with air that had been heated by passing over the engine. Motoring correspondents campaigned for years to have the radiator moved to the front of the car but it was not until 1997 that their wish was finally granted.

⋄ In the Money ⋄

Ken Burkitt, of Niagara Falls, Ontario, Canada, covered a 1969 Mini with thousands of gold-plated one-penny coins. To ensure a perfect fit, he bent the coins into shape with a vice and covered each coin with several coats of polyurethane to prevent discoloration or rust.

It was not the first coin-covered Mini, however. To promote the Beatles' single 'Penny Lane' in 1967, a Mini was covered in 14,000 old pennies.

⋄ Water, Water Everywhere ⋄

The water leaks which plagued the Mini in its early days — and which were found three months later to have been caused by the metal plates in the floor being lapped the wrong way — prompted one dissatisfied customer to write in to BMC and declare that he was only glad the company didn't build boats.

It wasn't just the floor of the car which got wet; the back seat cushion also had a tendency to become soaked in wet weather. One night, two BMC troubleshooters drove a Mini up the M1 to try and find the cause of the problem. They found that when the driver's window was opened in damp conditions, a fine spray was getting past the door seal and hitting the rear cushion. At the end of the journey, they found about four gallons of water in the rear cushion, making it so heavy that they could barely drag it out of the car.

In total, some 8,000 Minis throughout the world had to be repaired, which sometimes required BMC staff to journey abroad armed with sealing kits. In the Middle East, customers were particularly surprised to find BMC telling them that they had come to stop water getting into their Minis. 'What water?' they would ask. 'It hasn't rained here for 15 years!'

☙ Unlucky Strike ❧

On September 1, 1959, just six days after the Mini was introduced, production at BMC was halted by an unofficial strike.

❖ Girl Power ❖

As befits a car that became such a firm female favourite, the Mini's first outright international rally victory came with a woman driver at the wheel. Pat Moss had been taught to drive at the age of 11 by her elder brother Stirling in the family Jeep, but it was as a show jumper that she first made her name in the world of sport, triumphing at the 1950 Horse of the Year Show.

Switching to a different type of horsepower, she developed into one of the world's leading rally drivers in the early Sixties – and beyond question the best female rally driver of her day. When she first drove for BMC, she demanded the use of a company car and of a BMC truck converted into a horse box. She was one of the few women able to master the fearsome Austin Healey 3000 and would probably have won the 1961 RAC Rally had she not stopped to give Swedish driver Erik Carlsson a tyre. By way of compensation, they married two years later.

By then Moss had switched to the new Mini Cooper and finished a creditable seventh in class at the 1962 Monte Carlo Rally. Then five months later, with Ann Wisdom again beside her, Moss went to the Netherlands and won the Tulip Rally outright. Within a few months she had also won the Baden-Baden Rally in the same car, 737 ABL. However, these successes could not disguise her dislike of the Mini, which she described as 'twitchy, and pretty unruly on the limit,' and in 1963 she joined Ford.

❖ Cooper's Royalty ❖

In return for lending his name to the Mini Cooper and helping with its development, John Cooper received a royalty of £2 per car. When BMC became British Leyland, its boss Lord Stokes asked Cooper pointedly what he actually did. Cooper replied: 'I win world championships and go up to Longbridge once a week to wind up Issigonis.' Stokes was not amused and refused to renew the agreement with Cooper in 1971. The official BL line for the parting of the ways was that the Cooper name on the badge drove up the Mini's insurance premiums and adversely affected sales.

After an absence of nearly twenty years, the Mini Cooper returned in 1990 with leather seats, a bigger, more powerful engine, and alloy wheels. It sold in such numbers that it was soon accounting for more than 40 per cent of Mini production.

❖ A Trip to the Palace ❖

Alec Issigonis received his knighthood on August 27, 1969 – 10 years and a day after the Mini made its debut. Naturally he drove to Buckingham Palace in an Austin Mini

❖ That's Magic! ❖

At the press launch of the Austin Seven in August 1959, the sales team decided to emphasise the car's spaciousness. To the tune of 'That Old Black Magic', the Mini appeared on stage and a procession of people climbed out of it one by one. First came three of the biggest men the team had been able to find, followed by the wife of one of the sales executives cradling their baby, then one of her friends, and finally two huge dogs. Once everyone was on stage, they began unloading vast quantities of luggage – including two sets of golf clubs – which had been squeezed into every available corner of the Mini, placing each item before the audience like a conjuring trick.

❖ Twin Doors ❖

The Minivan had twin doors at the rear, not to facilitate access to the interior, but to save space on the BMC production line. The Minivan needed to be assembled on the standard nose-to-tail production line with its doors open, and the double-door arrangement saved approximately two feet of space on the production line behind each vehicle.

❈ Partially Sighted ❈

Towards the end of the 1967 1,000 Lakes Rally in his native Finland, Timo Makinen became concerned that his Mini Cooper was starting to overheat. So he decided to drive with the bonnet open and secured in place by a leather strap. But the relentless vibration from the bumpy roads caused the strap to break and the bonnet flew up, obliterating all but a tiny section of windscreen vision. Makinen knew there was no time to stop and, by slackening his seat belt, he was able to crane his neck around the raised bonnet and keep the car going at full speed, dropping just 19 seconds on his quickest rival. It was a hair-raising end to the rally but it proved worthwhile as he went on to win by eight seconds. If he had stopped to close the bonnet, he would have lost.

❈ Safety First ❈

'I make my cars with such good brakes, such good steering, that if people get into a crash it's their own fault.' – Sir Alec Issigonis

❖ A Different Corner ❖

While conducting a recce of the 1965 Alpine Rally route, Paddy Hopkirk and navigator Henry Liddon could not agree on the grading of a sharp left-hand turn on the Col du Granier, south of Chambery in France. Originally they rated it a 'medium left' before deciding to add the exclamation 'and how'. These notes were duly photocopied and passed on to the other members of the works Mini team. On the day of the actual rally, with Rauno Aaltonen approaching the contentious corner at full tilt, his co-driver Tony Ambrose tried to decipher Liddon's handwriting but mistakenly announced it as 'medium left and house'. Aaltonen was still frantically looking for the non-existent house when the Mini ran out of road and became airborne.

❖ An Uneasy Relationship ❖

Although the Morris Minor was the car that made Alec Issigonis's name, it received a frosty reception from Morris chief, Lord Nuffield. When he first saw the bulbous shape of the prototype Morris Minor, Nuffield snapped: 'We can't make that, it looks like a poached egg!'

In fact Nuffield had little time for Issigonis, and often referred to him as 'Issy wassy'. The two men are believed to have met only twice, firstly on the occasion of the unveiling of the Morris Minor prototype, and again in 1960 when Nuffield finally conceded that the Minor was a good design.

❖ Overseas Assembly ❖

In the mid-1960s, more than 5,000 Minis were being built every week. In those days, up to a third of all new BMC cars were sent off as CKD (kit) packs to places like Australia and South Africa, where final assembly would then take place.

❖ Design Icon ❖

Prompted by fashion guru Paul Smith's use of a Mini design on a range of skirts for his women's collection, Rover offered him his very own Mini. Mirroring the designs from his latest collection, he gave the car a highly distinctive look by decorating it with 84 stripes in 26 different colours. It went on display at the Tokyo Motor Show in October 1997.

Rover were so pleased with the results of the collaboration that the following year they issued a Paul Smith special edition production Mini. It featured handmade enamelled gold-plated badges on the bonnet and a smart black leather interior, but the most striking feature was the bodywork's shade of 'Paul Smith blue'. When asked by Rover what colour he had in mind for the car, Smith pointed to the shirt he was wearing and said, 'I want it like this.' He then handed over a piece of cloth from his shirt tail.

❖ Standing the Test of Time ❖

'The Mini has stood the test of time because it was so new when it came out and didn't rely on any gimmicks. It has always been strongly associated with the right people and places.' – Paul Smith

❖ Family Ties ❖

Bernd Pischetsrieder, the head of BMW in 1994 when that company acquired Rover and therefore the manufacture of the Mini, was a great nephew of Alec Issigonis.

❖ Something to Shout About ❖

Magazine advertisements for the Mini in 1976 featured Lulu (with obligatory Seventies perm) standing beside a shiny new Clubman. The accompanying copy began: 'Once upon a time, Lulu drove a Mini. And loved it so much she nearly cried when she sold it. Recently, we showed Lulu a new Mini Clubman. She said it was like falling in love all over again.'

❖ A Costly Error ❖

One of the earliest problems facing production workers was lining up the Mini's subframe with its body so that the screws that went through the turrets would always bite on to their threads. A number of subframes had to be scrapped before a solution was eventually found, and each time it happened, it cost £1 5s 0d – a sizeable chunk of the total cost of assembling the car.

❖ On the Slide ❖

Whilst increasing space and reducing cost, the Mini's sliding windows did hinder sales in hot countries because they offered little by way of ventilation. In the Caribbean, this led to the Ford Anglia enjoying considerable success at the expense of the Mini. In the basic Mini, the rear quarter windows (located alongside the rear seats) were fixed but on the De Luxe models they could be hinged outwards to provide at least a degree of ventilation. It was not until 1969 that the Mini began to feature wind-up windows.

❖ UK Mini Production Timeline ❖

(with original prices)

1959–67: Austin Se7en (from 1962 known as Austin Mini): 848cc £497 (basic), £537 (De Luxe)

1959–67: Morris Mini Minor: 848cc £497 (basic), £537 (De Luxe), £561 (Super De Luxe), £606 (De Luxe Automatic)

1960–61: Austin Se7en Countryman: 848cc £623

1960–67: Morris Mini Traveller Mk1: 848cc £532 (all metal body), £623 (wood framing)

1960–83: Austin Se7en/Morris Minivan (from 1969 known as Mini Van): 848cc (998cc from 1967) £360

1961–62: Austin Super Se7en: 848cc £592

1961–67: Austin Se7en Cooper, Austin and Morris Mini Cooper: 997cc £679

1961–83: Austin Mini Pick-Up and Morris Mini Pick-Up (from 1969 known as Mini Pick Up): 848cc (998cc from 1967) £360

1962–67: Austin Mini Countryman Mk1: 848cc £532 (all metal), £623 (wooden framing)

1963–64: Austin and Morris Cooper S: 1071cc £695

1964–65: Austin and Morris Mini Cooper S: 970cc £693

1964–67: Austin and Morris Mini Cooper S Mk1: 1275cc £778

1964–68: Austin and Morris Mini Moke: 848cc £405

1967–69: Austin Mini Mk II and Morris Mini Mk II: 848cc £509 (basic), £555 (848cc Super De Luxe), £579 (998cc Super De Luxe)

1967–69: Austin Mini Countryman Mk II and Morris Mini Traveller Mk II: 998cc £610 (all metal), £629 (wooden framing)

1967–69: Austin and Morris Mini Cooper Mk II: 998cc £631

1967–70: Austin and Morris Mini Cooper S Mk II: 1275cc £849

1969–70: Mini 850: 848cc £596

1969–80: Mini Clubman and Mini Clubman Estate: 998cc (1098cc from 1975) £720 (Mini Clubman), £763 (Mini Clubman Estate)

1969–80: Mini 1275 GT: 1275cc £834

1969–82: Mini 1000: 998cc £675

1970–71: Mini Cooper S Mk III: 1275cc £942

1976: Mini Limited Edition 1000: 998cc £1,406

1979: Mini 1100 Special: 1098cc £3,300

1979–80: Mini 850 City and Mini 850 Super De Luxe: 848cc £2,482

1980–92: Mini City: 998cc £2,796, £2,999 (Mini City E), £3,363 (1000HL Saloon)

1982–92: Mini Mayfair: 998cc £3,363

1983: Mini Sprite: 998cc £3,334

1984: Mini 25: 998cc £3,865

1985: Mini Ritz: 998cc £3,798

1986: Mini Chelsea: 998cc £3,898

1986: Mini Piccadilly: 998cc £3,928

1987: Mini Park Lane: 998cc £4,194

1987: Mini Advantage: 998cc £4,286

1988: Mini Red Hot and Mini Jet Black: 998cc £4,382

1988: Mini Designer: 998cc £4,654

1989: Mini Racing and Mini Flame: 998cc £4,795

1989: Mini Rose and Mini Sky: 998cc £4,695

1989: Mini 30: 998cc £5,599

1990–96: Rover Mini Cooper: 1275cc £6,595

1990: Mini Racing Green, Mini Flame Red and Mini Check Mate: 998cc £5,455

1990: Mini Studio 2: 998cc £5,375

1991–96: Rover Mini Cabriolet: 1275cc £11,995

1991: Mini Neon: 998cc £5,570

1992: Mini British Open Classic: 1275cc £7,195

1992: Mini Italian Job: 1275cc £5,995

1993: Mini Rio: 1275cc £5,495

1993: Mini Tahiti: 1275cc £5,795

1994: Mini Cooper Monte Carlo: 1275cc £7,995

1994: Mini 35: 1275cc £5,695

1994-96: Cooper Grand Prix (only 35 built): 1275cc £13,495

1995: Mini Sidewalk: 1275cc £5,895

1996: Mini Equinox: 1275cc £6,195

1996: Mini Cooper 35: 1275cc £8,195

1996–2000: Mini MPI: 1275cc £8,995

1996–2000: Mini Cooper MPI: 1275cc £8,995

1997: Mini Limo: 1275cc £50,000 (approx.)

1998: Rover Mini Paul Smith: 1275cc £10,225

1998: Mini Cooper Sports: 1275cc £10,525

1999: Mini Cooper S Touring: 1275cc £11,595

1999: Mini Cooper S Sport 5: 1275cc £13,650

1999: Mini Cooper S Works: 1275cc £12,495

1999: Rover Mini 40: 1275cc £10,995

1999: John Cooper LW: 1275cc £10,995

2000: Classic Mini Se7en: 1275cc £9,495

2000: Classic Cooper: 1275cc £9,895

2000: Classic Cooper Sport: 1275cc £10,895

❖ Big in Japan ❖

By the start of the 1990s, around 40 per cent of Rover's Mini production went to Japan, where small cars were hugely popular. The restricted headroom that was often the bane of tall European Mini drivers was never really a problem for the Japanese. In 1990 alone, more than 12,000 Minis were exported to Japan – nearly a 6,000 per cent increase on the figure of barely 200 from 10 years earlier. The demand even for second-hand Minis in Japan was so great that the depreciation was better than for a Mercedes. Mini owner clubs started up all over the country and when a Mini was entered in the 1994 Monte Carlo Rally, a Jumbo Jet had to be chartered just to fly all the Japanese fan club members to the event.

❖ That Sinking Feeling ❖

West Midlands rally enthusiast John Handley claimed to be the first person to buy a Mini for competition use. Having seen pre-launch photos of the Mini in newspapers and magazines, he decided that it was the ideal vehicle for rallying, and on the car's first day on sale, he persuaded his local agent, Darlaston Motor Services, to part with its sole demonstration model. That same day, he took it to a meeting of the

Hagley and District Light Car Club, but when he announced that he was planning to go rallying with it his friends roared with laughter. They did not see how a car that low on the ground could possibly survive a rally. Handley nobly ignored the jibes but started to think they might have had a point when, during the Mini's debut in the Worcestershire Rally, he suddenly noticed something moving in the passenger footwell. It was the rubber mat floating on rising water.

❖ Blunt Speaking ❖

Devotees of the classic Mini treated the 1969 arrival of the Clubman in much the same way as Pete Best fans greeted Ringo's installation as the Beatles' new drummer: in other words, as an unwanted interloper. It was the Clubman's blunt nose that so infuriated Mini purists, and John Bolster spoke for many when he wrote in *Autosport*: 'They have ruined the appearance, which is a great pity because the original car was completely functional and well proportioned. That awful Clubman bonnet would look very well on a Japanese car, but it clashes hopelessly with the shape of the rest of the body.' For good measure he added: 'They have also stuck boy racer stripes along the sides: just the thing to attract the attention of the police.'

❈ Perfect Parking ❈

'To me, the Mini is to parking what the British sandwich is to hunger – a perfect design classic.' – David Bowie

❈ A Much Travelled Car ❈

In 1964, the Mini Cooper 970 S acquired sporting homologation (achieved by proving that the competition car is based on a production model available for sale to the public) even though only one car had actually been made at that time. A BMC manager told the RAC that 1,000 cars had been produced, which meant that for the next few months that solitary car had to travel the length and breadth of the country – to appear in dealer showrooms and on racing circuits – to convince the RAC that a full quota had been manufactured.

❈ The Mini's Engine ❈

The A-Series engine was first used in 1951 in the 803cc Austin A30. One of the engine's key components was its highly efficient cylinder head, designed by independent consultant Harry Weslake, who discovered that a heart-shaped combustion area with a protruding strip between the inlet and exhaust valves allowed the gases to swirl and thereby produced a more efficient combustion of the mixture. This engine was incorporated in the A30 and the Morris Minor until 1956 when it was enlarged to 948cc and the cars were renamed the Austin A35 and Morris Minor 1000 respectively. When it came to building the Mini, Alec Issigonis eventually settled on an 848cc version of the A35/Minor engine.

❖ Minis in the Movies: The Top 10 ❖

1   *The Italian Job*
2   *Goodbye Pork Pie*
3   *Four Weddings and a Funeral*
4   *The Bourne Identity*
5   *Three Men and a Little Lady*
6   *51st State*
7   *Shallow Grave*
8   *Some Kind of Wonderful*
9   *A Room for Romeo Brass*
10   *Doctor in Distress*

Whilst *The Italian Job* marks the Mini's most celebrated screen role, the car has also played a part in countless other films. Hugh Grant jumped into one and got to the church on time in *Four Weddings and a*

Funeral; Matt Damon jumped into one and got away in *The Bourne Identity*; Tom Selleck swapped a Ferrari for a Mini Cooper and, squashed behind the wheel, raced around the English countryside in *Three Men and a Little Lady*; a kilt-wearing Samuel L. Jackson drove a 1982 Mini Cooper in *51st State*; in *Doctor in Distress*, Dirk Bogarde made the mistake of parking his Mini in the space reserved for his new boss's car; two Austin Minis were seen frozen in time in *101 Dalmatians*; a pair of Minis featured in a stock car race in *On Her Majesty's Secret Service*; Ewan McGregor drove a dark green Mini Cooper in *Shallow Grave*; Mini-driving tomboy Watts (played by Mary Stuart Masterson) developed romantic urges for best friend Keith (Eric Stoltz) in the 1987 movie *Some Kind of Wonderful*; a green Mini van featured heavily in Shane Meadows' 1999 film *A Room for Romeo Brass*; a six-seater Mini appeared in another Shane Meadows movie, *Once Upon a Time in the Midlands*, starring Robert Carlyle – not to mention Mini supporting roles in the likes of *Ring of Bright Water*, *Alfie*, *The Fast Lady*, *Billy Liar*, *Sid and Nancy*, *In the Name of the Father*, *The Eiger Sanction*, *The Avengers*, *A View to a Kill*, *On Her Majesty's Secret Service*, *Hotel Rwanda*, *Confessions of a Driving Instructor*, *Clockwise*, *Get Carter*, *The Man who Knew Too Little*, *Lara Croft: Tomb Raider*, *Forget Paris*, *Bridget Jones's Diary* (covered in snow), and *The Wicker Man* (as a police car).

In a 1981 New Zealand 'road movie' *Goodbye Pork Pie*, a teenager enjoyed a serious of escapades in a rented yellow Mini named Pork Pie. This is believed to be the only movie where the name of the starring Mini appears in the title.

❖ A Simple Ironmonger ❖

Alec Issigonis famously hated the word 'style' in relation to the Mini, maintaining that its much-loved shape was dictated solely by the car's required capacity. 'It is a functional thing,' he once said. 'A car should take its shape entirely from the engineering that goes into it.' However, he did add of the Mini: 'The thing that satisfied me most was that it looked like no other car.'

When, on his eightieth birthday, in 1986, somebody asked him if he thought of himself as an engineer, a scientist or an architect, he replied simply: 'An ironmonger.'

❖ Partners and Mascots ❖

In Denmark, the Mini was known as the Austin Partner (1959-64) and the Morris Mascot (1961-81).

❖ Broadspeed Retro Minis ❖

Founded by Ralph Broad in 1962, Broadspeed Engineering, of Sparkbrook, Birmingham, specialised in performance engine tuning, and Team Broadspeed went on to race Mini Coopers with considerable success. By the 1990s the company had moved to Colchester and was concentrating on creating customised retro Minis, combining modern features with the traditional 1960s look of all things Mini from Coopers to pickups. One of their most spectacular creations was a 1966 GT Coupé that attached a sporty rear section to the Mini front and became known as the 'Mini Aston Martin'.

Over 1,000 Broadspeed Minis have been exported to some 40 countries worldwide, including a highly modified Mini Cooper S 'Woody' Countryman that was commissioned by Roy Disney, nephew of Walt.

❖ The Lord Giveth ❖

BMC boss Leonard Lord has been described as the godfather of the Mini. Although he looked unassuming – with spectacles, and a cigarette permanently lodged in the corner of his mouth – he was known as a real corporate bruiser whose motto was: 'If the door is not open, then you kick it open.' His first job was as a draughtsman at Courtaulds, where one of the directors asked him what his ambition was. 'To sit in your chair,' replied Lord.

In 1923, he joined the Morris Motor Company and was promoted to general manager nine years later. Differences of opinion with William Morris led to Lord moving to Morris's great rival, Austin, in 1938, and he went on to become BMC managing director following the merger of the two companies. When he was knighted in 1954, he took the title of Lord Lambury, remarking with characteristic bluntness that 'Lord Lord would sound bloody stupid.' He retired as managing director in 1956 at the age of 60, handing over to George Harriman, but remained as BMC chairman until his sixty-fifth birthday. Harriman respected his old boss so much that he left Lord's office untouched and unoccupied until his death in 1967.

❖ Diddy Mini ❖

Fulham Football Club match day announcer and radio and TV presenter 'Diddy' David Hamilton drives a red Mini Cooper with the registration plate D1 DDY. He bought the personalised plate for £5,000 in 1990 and says it matches not only his nickname but the personality of the car itself. 'It looks cute, and people can't help saying so. It's been a great publicity tool for me over the years.'

He often finds notes stuck to the windscreen asking him if he will sell the plate. Interested parties have included French footballer Didier Deschamps and a woman by the name of Diddy McDonald.

❖ A Car For Everyone ❖

'I never thought the car would last 41 years, but everyone has had one, from royalty downwards.' – BMC chief draughtsman Jack Daniels, 2000

❖ Beetle Crushed ❖

In August 1959 – the month the Mini was launched – the Volkswagen Beetle passed three million total sales. Despite an infamously noisy engine which could drown out a low-flying 707, it was a big seller in the United States as well as in Europe. Both the Mini and the Beetle produced 34bhp, but the Mini extracted it from only 850cc, compared to the German car's 1200cc. The Beetle's top speed of 68mph was four short of the Mini's maximum, and yet the VW cost £700 – over £200 more than the Mini. The British, as ever, liked value for money.

Capitalising on the rivalry between the two cars, England's York Raceway stages an annual Mini vs Beetle shootout along a quarter-mile drag strip, with the Mini's superior acceleration to the VW usually proving decisive.

❖ Fall Guy ❖

Tony Fall, who drove Mini Coopers with great success in the 1960s, was encouraged to get into rally driving while working as a junior salesman at Appleyards car dealership in Leeds. Ian Appleyard had won the Alpine Rally three times in the 1950s in a Jaguar and he allowed Fall to borrow the company's Mini Cooper demonstrator from the showroom for weekend competition. The car was then polished up and put back on display every Monday morning.

❖ The World's Fastest Mini? ❖

The short length of a Mini would hardly appear to lend itself to drag racing but each year the British Mini Club stages the British Mini Showdown, a quarter-mile drag race at the Shakespeare County Raceway, near Long Marston, Warwickshire. Over 300 competitors take part, and in 2008 Nathan Dobson flew down the track in just 9.961sec in his Mini... helped in no small part by a 7.3 litre Chevrolet engine.

❖ Tiger in the Tank ❖

Wales-based artist and former psychiatric nurse Torsten Baumbach spent nearly three months covering his Mini in tiger print fur. To complete the illusion, he even attached a tail to the boot lid.

❖ A Fistful of Sand ❖

In early Minis, oil tended to leak on to the clutch plate from the main crankshaft oil seal. Rally drivers overcame this problem by throwing handfuls of sand into the clutch housing — sometimes it was the only way they could finish a stage.

❖ Police Misinformant ❖

Back in the 1960s, it was a widely accepted fact that if you wanted to know the time or needed directions, you asked a policeman. So when the Mini Cooper S team of Rauno Aaltonen and Tony Ambrose approached a junction near Bonneville on the 1965 French Alpine Rally, at which they had turned right on the pre-rally reconnaissance but where a helpful gendarme was now telling them to go left, they understandably followed the advice of the man in uniform. It was their misfortune to have stumbled across a distant relative of Inspector Clouseau because, on following his directions, they became temporarily lost. They saw through his ineptitude fairly quickly and were soon able to return to the correct route, but the minute they lost in doing so was enough to deprive them of any chance of victory.

❖ You've Been Mini'd ❖

The Mini's ability to hurtle around corners, zip away from traffic lights and scythe through heavy traffic – advertisements proclaimed that the Mini was better in a jam than strawberries – prompted many letters to newspapers about irresponsible driving. *The Motor* highlighted the situation, writing in 1960 that 'far from needing to feel apologetic about his rate of progress in a modern main-road traffic stream, the Mini Minor owner is far more likely to be irked by bigger cars getting in his way.' All of which caused owners of larger cars to resent the little upstart, a state of affairs not helped by stickers which began to appear in rear windows declaring, 'You've Just Been Mini'd.'

❖ Like The Tardis ❖

'The Mini is like Dr Who's Tardis – as small as a phone box outside, as big as the Albert Hall inside.'
– John Cooper

❖ Lost in Translation ❖

When young Swedish driver Jorma Lusenius came to Britain to drive a Mini at the 1965 RAC Rally, BMC competitions manager Stuart Turner assigned him Mike Wood as co-driver. Since Lusenius's knowledge of English was as tenuous as Wood's grasp of Swedish, Turner sent the pair away on a bonding session in Wales. Beforehand, Wood prepared a few useful phrases and asked Timo Makinen to translate them into Swedish. However the mischievous Makinen deliberately put the translations in a different order to the original phrases, with the result that 'sharp turn right' could have sounded to Swedish ears as 'how do you like your eggs?' In the circumstances, Lusenius and Wood did remarkably well to finish sixth.

❖ The Innocenti Minis: The First Italian Job ❖

Best known for its manufacture of the Mods' favourite motor scooter – the Lambretta – the Innocenti motor factory in Milan had first linked up with BMC in 1960 to produce the Austin A40 Farina and the partnership was cemented in 1965 when the first Mini Coopers were built in Italy. Initially, the principal differences from the British-made Mini Cooper were that the Italian car had wind-up door windows, side indicator lamps and reversing lamps, although the general consensus of opinion was that the interior of the Innocenti was also superior, boasting a wider range of instruments on the dashboard.

The success of *The Italian Job* did much to popularise the Mini in Italy, and between 1966 and 1974 more than 50,000 Minis a year were produced at the Milan plant, sometimes at a rate of 300 cars a day. The Innocenti Mini Cooper, which, despite being less powerful than the 1275 S, still boasted a top speed of 95mph, was never officially sold in the UK, but a number were imported privately.

❖ Finding Fault ❖

'The evident effort which has been made to please the public in these practical ways makes it all the more extraordinary that with three interior lights, actuated by three separate switches, it remains impossible for either the driver or front-seat passenger to read at night, and with the front seats fully back the ash tray is so far away as to be inaccessible to all but apes, few of whom normally travel in motorcars and a great majority of whom are, I am instructed, non-smokers.' – *The Motor* of January 1960 praised the Mini's spaciousness and safety but found fault elsewhere

❖ Race Ace Mini Owners ❖

The Mini has always been hugely popular with motoring aficionados and racing drivers. Steve McQueen and Paul Newman, famous for their love of fast cars and motor racing, both owned a Mini as did motor racing legends Graham Hill, John Surtees, Jackie Stewart, Bruce McLaren, Jack Brabham, Niki Lauda and James Hunt. Diminutive Formula One supremo Bernie Ecclestone also once owned a Mini.

Perhaps most remarkably of all, one giant of the sports car world owned no fewer than three Minis – Enzo Ferrari. The founder of what is the most famous sports car company in the world loved to escape from the stresses of big business by driving his Minis around the mountain roads near his company's base at Maranello in Italy. BMC also made him an automatic version and generously drove it all the way out to Italy, only to realise when they got there that they had forgotten to convert it to left-hand drive. In the circumstances, Ferrari politely declined the present.

❖ Sales Rocket ❖

After Paddy Hopkirk's sensational victory in the 1964 Monte Carlo Rally, BMC reported that sales of the Mini for the first quarter of that year were up 53 per cent compared with the first quarter of the previous year.

❖ Not Too Cheap ❖

'If you build bloody good cars, they'll sell themselves.' – BMC chairman Leonard Lord, responding to criticism that BMC was cutting its own throat with its original pricing of the Mini

❖ My Baby Mini ❖

There is no doubt that the small, rounded – almost cheeky – shape of the Mini contributed enormously to its success. For a start, it brought out the maternal instinct in women, who would lovingly refer to their Mini as 'their baby.' As late as the mid 1980s, Rover were focussing on the human aspect of the car with their TV advertising campaign 'Minis have feelings too.'

Nevertheless shortly after conception, Italian designer Pinin Farina suggested to Issigonis that the car should be restyled. To which Issigonis replied, with commendable foresight: 'Look at your cars, they're like women's clothes — out of date in two years. My car will still be in fashion after I've gone.'

❖ The McLaren Minis ❖

Before founding the McLaren team, New Zealander Bruce McLaren was Jack Brabham's junior partner in the all-conquering Cooper Formula One set-up, and by virtue of his victory at the 1959 United States Grand Prix, the 22-year-old became the youngest driver at that time to win a Formula One Grand Prix. He was also an enthusiastic racer of Mini Coopers. For the New Zealand Grand Prix meeting at Ardmore in January 1962, McLaren was hurriedly given one of the first Mini Coopers off the UK production line, there being just five days to tune the car prior to shipment to New Zealand. By 1963 he had imported a green and white Mini Cooper S for racing, and this was later owned by his father Les and used as the family's second car. In January of that year, Bruce won the Teretonga

International race on New Zealand's South Island in a Cooper F1 car, and also thrilled spectators with some hair-raising drives in his Mini Cooper in supporting saloon car races. He didn't believe in taking things easy. Even while doing a series of exploratory laps – with Innes Ireland as his passenger – McLaren managed to lose a right front wheel and end up in the sand hills at the side of the track.

⸙ Join the Club ⸙

There are thousands of Mini clubs throughout the world, including dozens in the UK, clubs in virtually every state in the US, Canada, Australia, New Zealand, Argentina, Belgium, Denmark, Austria, Spain, Netherlands, France, Germany, Greece, Italy, Japan, Malaysia, Portugal, South Africa, Russia, Ukraine, Sweden, Thailand, Switzerland, Slovenia, South Korea and Trinidad & Tobago.

⸙ The Mincia ⸙

Among the many mutant Minis in existence is Robin Cooke's Mincia. It has the body of a Mini Clubman 1275 GT fitted with a 1600cc Lancia Beta engine. The result gives 153bhp, a top speed of 115mph and 0-60mph in 5.7 seconds.

❖ Mr Bean Does A Road Test ❖

'Driving a Mini Cooper is not like driving in the real world. It's more like driving in a comic strip because of the extraordinary way in which the car responds to your every twitch and twiddle: you point the wheel and it just goes. No delay, no lurch, no body roll, just ZZIPPP! And you're facing another direction. If you brake, the car appears to be instantly going slower. No dive, no fuss, just the feeling that an unseen hand has gone WHHOAHH!.... Once you are bowling along, fun can be had by the spadeful. Apart from its neo-perfect basic design and proportions, nearly all its joyful wieldiness can be attributed to its smallness. It is a titchy little thing. Despite not having had any real development money spent on it in thirty years, this 10ft bundle of joy remains the strongest argument extant in favour of really small cars.' – Rowan Atkinson assesses the new Mini Cooper in the November 1991 issue of *Car Magazine*

❖ 'Smokey' Rhodes ❖

The legendary leader of the works John Cooper Mini team in the British Saloon Car Championship in the mid-1960s was John Rhodes, who acquired the nickname 'Smokey' from an unorthodox driving style that saw him create a dense smoke screen at every corner from the scorching inside front wheel as he flung the Mini sideways into the turn. Rhodes had previously driven various single-seaters including a Formula One Cooper, but it was in the Mini Cooper that he made his name.

'Having just jumped out of an F1 car,' he recalled, 'the Mini Cooper speed did not impress. Neither did the brakes, but who needs brakes! Lift the throttle, the car would oversteer; floor the throttle and one could power into a superb drift in clouds of tyre smoke. Wonderful!'

'Smokey' Rhodes's technique of virtually ignoring the brake pedal not only temporarily blinded his immediate pursuers but his sideways approach to a bend also made it difficult for anyone to overtake him on the way into a corner. The tactic helped him to win the 1300cc class of the British Saloon Car Championship four years in a row between 1965 and 1968. The only problem was that his tyre temperatures often reached 130 degrees Centigrade – 30 degrees above boiling point, and at a time when even Formula One racing tyres were not expected to cope with anything in excess of 100 degrees.

❖ Mini Tour ❖

One of the first Minis to leave the production line was loaned to *Autocar* motoring writer Ronald Barker who set off with a colleague on a long-distance trip to test the endurance and durability of the new little car. They covered 8,197 miles around the Mediterranean, reporting on their trip over four issues of the magazine.

Their longest daytime drive took them 506 miles from Benghazi to Misurata in one day, averaging over 53mph. The fastest part of their journey was in Libya where they covered 82 miles in just 74 minutes. In Turkey, they travelled 662 miles over a 24-hour period, managing all of this, of course, without the aid of modern motorways. Over the whole adventure, they used 228 gallons of petrol, an average of 36mpg, which would be a respectable fuel consumption figure even today, 50 years later.

❖ Adam Adamant Lives! ❖

Frozen in time in a block of ice since 1902 by his arch enemy 'The Face', suave Edwardian adventurer Adam Adamant (played by actor Gerald Harper) was brought back to life for the 1966 BBC TV series *Adam Adamant Lives!* Finding himself in the heart of Swinging London, his chosen mode of transport was naturally a Radford Mini de Ville GT, registration AA 1000.

Also in the 1960s, Patrick McGoohan (as special agent John Drake in ITV's *Danger Man*) would sit behind the wheel of a 1963 Austin Mini Cooper 1071 S (registration HOP 731) in hot pursuit of villains who drove much faster cars such as Mercedes-Benz 190 Fintails. What appeared an unequal contest was always turned on its head thanks to the resourcefulness of Drake and his Mini.

Proof that the Mini was still in vogue in the late 1970s came when Wendy Craig's frustrated housewife Ria Parkinson drove a Mini with a Union Jack roof around town in search of fulfilment in Carla Lane's BBC sitcom *Butterflies*.

Minis have appeared in numerous other TV series, from *Monty Python* to *Little Britain*, *The Persuaders* to *Midsomer Murders*, *The Saint* to *Heartbeat*, and *The Likely Lads* to *Friends*.

❖ A Pleasant Surprise ❖

'When the Mini was designed and into production, I never gave competition motoring a single thought. We were preoccupied in the design with getting good roadholding and stability, but for safety reasons, and to give the driver more pleasure. It never occurred

to me that this thing would turn out to be such a
successful rally car.' – Alec Issigonis

❖ Export Markets ❖

On the Mini's twenty-fifth birthday – in 1984 – its
major export markets were: France (6,861), Germany
(2,988), Italy (2,053), Netherlands (1,704), Belgium
(1,625), Japan (821), Ireland (629), Portugal (543)
and South Africa (312).

❖ Mini Mayfair ❖

To emphasise the point that the little Mini appealed
to all classes of society, the Mini Mayfair was launched
in 1982 and, as a publicity gimmick, was posed in
a posh Mayfair apartment. The car itself came with
radio, head restraints, locking fuel cap and tinted
glass fitted as standard. From 1984, it also had front
disc brakes and 12-inch wheels.

❖ Nursing the Cooper ❖

Although the powerful Mini Cooper S was designed
primarily for competition, BMC demanded that it
should also be suitable for everyday driving. The
compromise achieved by creating a car that was not

only quick but could cope well with heavy town traffic did not please everyone. BMC competitions manager Stuart Turner later remarked that the Mini Cooper S would have been a much better sports saloon 'if Sales hadn't insisted that it be usable by the district nurse'!

❖ Lady Racer ❖

Just as Pat Moss was the leading lady Mini rally driver, so Christabel Carlisle used to hammer the little car around the racing circuits of Britain and Europe in the early 1960s. An aristocratic piano teacher from South Kensington, she caught the speed bug when her family bought her a Mini in 1960 for her twenty-first birthday. She competed in a few rallies just for fun but after going to Brands Hatch with friends, she was so unimpressed that she vowed the only way she would ever go racing again would be if she was driving. True to her word, she entered her 848cc Mini (CMC 77) at Silverstone but put the car into the straw bales at Copse.

She recalled that the early appearances of Minis at race meetings would prompt laughter from spectators and fellow drivers alike... but how the joke quickly wore off as the Minis began passing larger cars at will.

Her first full season's racing was 1961, when she performed creditably, finishing second at Brands Hatch on October 1 – a place ahead of none other than Steve McQueen who was enjoying a break from filming in Britain. For the following year she was given a 997cc Mini Cooper by the BMC factory although she was not part of the works team.

Over the next two seasons she continued to race with distinction, regularly excelling in her class, but it all turned sour at Silverstone on July 20, 1963 during a support race for the final round of the British Saloon Car Championship. Driving an Austin Healey Sprite, she spun at Woodcote and hit the pit wall just as a marshal was walking in front of it with his back to the oncoming cars. The marshal sustained fatal injuries and Carlisle was badly concussed. Although absolved of any blame, she never raced again.

In 1965, she married Sir James Andrew Watson and became Lady Watson. At the age of 50, she climbed Mount Gondogora in the Himalayas and in 1999 she marked her sixtieth birthday by walking from one end of Britain to the other.

❖ The Typical Mini Driver ❖

In the 1990s, Rover carried out a survey to try and define the typical Mini driver, only to find that there was no such thing. Its study concluded that 70 per cent of Minis were bought by women; 56 per cent of Mini owners were married; 13 per cent were younger than 24; 16 per cent were older than 65; and the main use for the Mini was as a second car to be driven in the city.

❖ Low Mileage ❖

In 2009, Rick Terrell, from Longview, Washington, USA, was able to offer for sale a 1962 Austin Seven Countryman 'Woody' that had only 36,000 miles on the clock – an average of about 1,000 miles for every year of its life. That's the equivalent of making nothing more than two return journeys from Plymouth to London a year. He bought it in England in 2005 when it had done just 34,000 miles. Apparently the reason for the low mileage and the car's immaculate condition was that the previous owner had kept it in a garage most of the time.

❖ South African Hybrid ❖

Built in South Africa between 1967 and 1969, the Wolseley 1000 was essentially a cross between a Mk I and a Mk II Mini with a Wolseley Hornet front end. It looked like an ordinary Mini but had a Wolseley grille badge, along with wind-down windows, a 998cc engine and hydrolastic suspension. Only around 450 were built, and they became much sought-after, none more so than by American-based enthusiast Chuck Heleker who bought one while on a trip to South Africa in 2000. He then had the car shipped to Port Miami, Florida, and for the next three weeks, he drove it over 6,000 miles across the United States to his home in Seattle.

❖ Star of the Palladium ❖

Fresh from its historic triumph at the 1964 Monte Carlo Rally, Paddy Hopkirk's Mini was photographed in Paris with the Beatles. Then it was shipped back to London to star in the most popular TV entertainment show of the day, *Sunday Night at the London Palladium*. On stage, the little car was hoisted on to a fixed podium with the drivers standing alongside. A second platform – the famous revolve which featured at the end of every show – carried host Bruce Forsyth, the high-kicking Tiller Girls, and the rest of the line-up, including comedian Tommy Cooper and singer Kathy Kirby. The audience responded by standing up and launching into a rousing rendition of 'Rule Britannia'.

Even when the Minis were robbed of victory in 1966, they appeared on stage at the Palladium. Host

Jimmy Tarbuck introduced them with the words: 'Ladies and gentlemen, we have brought you many famous people at the London Palladium, stars of stage and screen, but tonight we are bringing you something you have never seen before – the *real* winners of the Monte Carlo Rally.'

Tarbuck then asked the driver of the first Mini home, Timo Makinen: 'Did you really need those lights?'

To which Makinen replied: 'I could have won it with a bunch of glow worms on the front!'

❖ The Stimson Scorcher ❖

First produced in the UK in 1976, the Stimson Scorcher – designed by Portsmouth-based Barry Stimson – was a three-wheeler that was powered by an Austin Mini engine and also used a Mini subframe and gearbox. The body was made from fibreglass and was usually completely open, offering the driver a minimum amount of protection against the elements.

It had a top speed of 100mph and could seat three people, but because it was classed as a motorcycle-sidecar combination, the third person didn't need to wear a crash helmet on UK roads. It was sold as a kit, and around thirty Scorchers were made before production ceased in 1980.

Stimson has long specialised in designing quirky cars, including the six-wheeled Safari Six, which also had a Mini front subframe and engine along with fibreglass bodywork in a spaceframe chassis.

The Scorcher and the Safari Six followed on from Stimson's 1970 creation, the Mini Bug, a doorless, roofless two-seater with a one-piece plastic body and a steel chassis into which working parts of an old Mini could be bolted. The Mini Bug sold so well as a kit car that British Leyland were interested in selling it through their Unipart division. However, Stimson rather blew it when he met BL managers. He recalled: 'They wanted to know all about the stress tests we'd put the car through. I said we had a fat friend and we got him to bounce up and down on the chassis; if it bent, we welded another strut in. My partner kicked me under the table and the Leyland people were not amused. We never got the deal.'

❖ On a High ❖

As a publicity stunt to demonstrate the durability of his caravans, Sam Alper – head of International Caravans – towed his famous Sprite caravan by Mini to an altitude of over 10,000ft. in Spain's Sierra Nevada Granada mountain range in 1973.

⋇ External Seams ⋇

When the Mini was first produced there was so little money available that BMC could not afford to build the body up on jigs. So the Mini was given its familiar external seams – visible on the outside of the car running down the A and C pillars and between the body and the floor pan – which allowed the body to be spot welded together without the aid of a jig.

⋇ Lauda's First Steps ⋇

Future Formula One World Champion Niki Lauda's first success in competition was at the wheel of a Mini Cooper. Yet the relationship did not exactly start promisingly as after trading in his Volkswagen to buy one, he promptly crashed the Mini on its first outing after skidding on ice in Vienna. He managed to repair it and soon swapped it for racing driver Felix Baumgartner's competitive 1275cc Mini Cooper S. Knowing that his parents disapproved of his intention to go racing, 19-year-old Lauda left the Baumgartner marking on the Mini and told his father that he was only storing it for his friend. Taking part in a hill climb at Mühlbacken on April 15, 1968, Lauda finished third in the first heat before winning the second, giving him second place overall.

Unfortunately, his exploits appeared in the local newspaper, and when his father read about them, he once again tried to stop him racing. History tells us that his pleas fell on deaf ears.

❖ The Long Mini ❖

When a 20-ft (6m) long, 12-seater, Cowley-built Mini was displayed in a Piccadilly showroom as a publicity gimmick for Christmas 1964, seven people rang to place orders. The idea probably inspired the BMW MINI XXL of 2004 – a 20-ft-long car with four doors, a passenger compartment with TV, DVD and phone, and a Jacuzzi!

❖ Who Do You Think You Are – Stirling Moss? ❖

In its early days the Mini needed all the friends it could get and so BMC were happy to oblige Stirling Moss when he asked if he could take one for a spin around the quiet lanes of the Lickey Hills. With Moss not exactly a stranger to accidents, it should have come as no surprise when he returned from his jaunt with a buckled engine compartment sustained in a head-on crash. Unperturbed, Alec Issigonis concentrated on the positives by telling Moss that the transverse location of the Mini's engine had acted as a safety device. Whereas with longitudinal mounting, such an impact might have caused the steering column to crush the driver, he said the transverse engine meant that the shock of the collision was absorbed and thus the crumpling of the car reduced. Moss's response was not recorded.

❖ Special Edition ❖

In 1976, the Mini became the first British car to produce a special edition – the Mini1000 Special. Priced at £1,406, it came in Brooklands Green and featured a gold waist coachline, twin chrome door mirrors and reclining front seats. As befitted the dubious fashions of the day, the interior had an orange-striped brushed nylon seat trim from the MGB range and dark orange 'safari' carpets. A total of 3,000 Mini 1000 Specials were sold in the UK.

❖ Back to the Monte ❖

To mark the thirtieth anniversary of his epic victory at the 1964 Monte Carlo Rally, 60-year-old Paddy Hopkirk was persuaded to drive one of the new 1275cc Mini Coopers in the 1994 event. Rover was even granted the registration L33 EJB in recognition of Hopkirk's 1964 car, 33 EJB, and the same car number, 37. Asked by *Top Gear*'s Tony Mason how the two cars compared, Hopkirk replied: 'The new one holds the road a lot better – you can actually go round corners a lot faster. But the steering's very heavy – you've got to hang on to it and you've got to do a lot of steering. It has 15 per cent more horsepower than the 1964 car, but the big difference is the 13-inch wheels instead of the little 10-inch.'

❖ Sketches on a Tablecloth ❖

Finnish rally driver Rauno Aaltonen was one of the sport's great thinkers. He was always looking for ways of getting better performance from the Mini Coopers and was known to sketch out his desired modifications on the white tablecloth of a restaurant where he was having dinner.

❖ In Loving Memory ❖

'For many people, the Mini was the first car that they owned. However many cars they subsequently get through, I doubt they will be remembered with the same care and affection as the Mini. It's a classy little classless car.' – Sir Terence Conran

❖ Minis Reunited ❖

Mini fans looking to find out what has happened to their long-lost cars can now do so via a website, Minis Reunited (www.minireunited.com).

❖ Day Trippers ❖

All four Beatles owned Minis, the most famous being George Harrison's psychedelic version which appeared in their 1967 film *Magical Mystery Tour*. Built by Harold Radford (Coachbuilder) Ltd in 1965, Austin Cooper S LGF 695D was originally black but was painted in psychedelic colours in 1967 using ideas from an art book. George also had a wall of his house painted in the same style, much to the annoyance of his neighbours. It was in that Mini that George, John, Cynthia Lennon and Patti Boyd apparently had their first LSD trip after leaving the home of a friend who had slipped it into their tea. George recalled driving very slowly because they didn't know what was happening to them. After *Magical Mystery Tour*, the car was given to Eric Clapton, but George got it back in the 1970s, lovingly maintained it and showed it at Goodwood as recently as 1998, three years before his death.

John Lennon bought his wife Cynthia a Mini in 1964 but because he didn't pass his driving test until 1965, he waited until then before getting a black Radford-built Austin Cooper S (LGF 696D). The following year he told a journalist: 'I decided I'd been a bit extravagant and bought too many cars, so I put the Ferrari and the Mini up for sale. Then one of the accountants said I was all right, so I got the cars back.' On August 28, 1967, Lennon arrived at Apple Studios in his Radford Mini after hearing of the death of the Beatles' manager Brian Epstein.

In 1965, Paul McCartney acquired a sage green Radford Mini Cooper S (GGJ 382C), which boasted rear lights from the Aston Martin factory, black leather interior, inside map lighting and a sunroof. He drove the Mini to Primrose Hill, North London, in early 1967 and saw a strange man walking about. This was the inspiration for his song 'The Fool On The Hill.' The car now resides in a Florida museum.

Ringo Starr owned Radford Austin Mini Cooper S LLO 836D. The Beatles' manager Brian Epstein bought it originally in 1966 and the next owner shown in the logbook is Richard Starkey, who took possession of it on June 15, 1967. Epstein had an arrangement with dealer Terry Doran to get cars for the Beatles at trade prices. Doran is the 'man from the motor trade' referred to in 'She's Leaving Home' on the Sergeant Pepper album.

❖ Mini Convoy ❖

On May 11, 2008, during the International Mini Meeting, a total of 884 Minis paraded through Lelystad, the Netherlands, breaking the Guinness world record for the largest ever convoy of Minis. This shattered the previous record of 310 Minis that took part in the 2007 Mini Grand Tour in North Devon between Westward Ho! and Ilfracombe.

❖ The Future's Bright ❖

Owners have done all manner of weird and wonderful things to their Minis – turning them into camper vans, sports cars, buggies, three-wheelers, six-wheelers, coupés, and even a hovercraft. For advertising purposes, one was fitted with a Ford back axle and a tubular steel frame and converted into a giant driveable can of Duckham's Q20-50.

But few can compare with the Outspan Orange.

Between 1972 and 1974, Brian Waite Ltd of Bodiam, East Sussex, converted half a dozen Minis into big round oranges, which were subsequently used in advertising campaigns all over Europe. They had a Mini automatic transmission unit with the gearchange on the driver's right, and entry was through a door at the rear of the orange. The super fruit had a top speed of 30mph – any faster it would roll over and, in view of its shape, probably for quite a long way.

Unlikely as it may sound, the Outspan Orange has taken part in the Historic Commercial Vehicle Society's London to Brighton run, frequently pipping other competitors to the finish... except on the occasions it ran out of juice. One of the original crop is believed to be in South Africa while another resides at the National Motor Museum at Beaulieu, Hampshire.

❖ Looking for an Excuse ❖

'By the time the team came to the end of the event there was a certain amount of disbelief among the organisers that the Group One Minis could have been so quick. The pressure then was such that I am sure they would have disqualified us for the colour of Paddy's socks if they could.' – BMC works team manager Stuart Turner on the controversial 1966 Monte Carlo Rally

❖ Seeing the Light ❖

The official reason given for the disqualification of the three Mini Coopers at the 1966 Monte Carlo Rally was that the Federation Internationale de l'Automobile in Paris ruled that the cars' iodine quartz headlights were not standard. The French Citroën that was named the eventual winner was, by contrast, declared legal because its bulbs were fitted as standard on some models. Amid the subsequent uproar, a private run-off was arranged between a standard Mini Cooper and the rally car, with Timo Makinen (who had finished first before disqualification) and a French journalist switching from car to car to highlight any differences. To emphasise the folly of the Minis' disqualification, the standard car actually proved faster than the rally car. Although this test had no effect on the result of the Monte, it did give Cooper S owners the satisfaction of knowing that their road car was quicker than Paddy Hopkirk's!

Yet the French authorities' decision was arguably not the worst of that era. Back in 1959, two cars had made the Mini's first venture overseas to compete in a Portuguese rally. Come the final reckoning, all of the leading cars – which in those early days did not include the Minis but nevertheless consisted of vehicles all foreign to Portugal – were disqualified for the heinous crime of wearing their numbers in the wrong colour, thereby allowing Portuguese entrants to be promoted to the victory podium in a shameless exhibition of nationalism.

❖ A Load of Crystal Balls ❖

Just like the music executive who rejected the Beatles and the journalist who predicted that *Coronation Street* would never last, not everyone foresaw a rosy future for the Mini. Three months after its launch, a member of the public, Mr G. Davies, wrote to *Autocar*:

'I really cannot understand why BMC have produced a glorified bubble car which costs nearly £500. Surely it would have been better to have spent the enormous amount of capital wasted on this in reducing the price of the A35, which was a real motor car. In my opinion this overpowered vehicle with scooter-like wheels and its most unnecessarily complicated front-wheel drive cannot hope to compete with orthodox cars which can be purchased with very little more money.'

❖ The Mini Marcos ❖

Founded by businessman Jem Marsh and aeronautical engineer Frank Costin in Trowbridge, Wiltshire, (using the first three letters from each surname) Marcos started building cars in 1959. Among the company's early customers was Jackie Stewart who gained his first racing experience at the wheel of a Marcos. In 1966, by which time Costin had moved on to pastures new, the company introduced the Mini Marcos, a fibreglass-bodied sports car built over Mini subframes. Despite being rather unfairly described by one correspondent as 'ugly as hell', the Mini Marcos made its name at the 1966 Le Mans 24 Hours Race, where it was the only British car to finish.

This kept sales ticking over nicely for a few years and although they eventually fell away, the Mini Marcos was reintroduced in 1991, and marked its resurrection by winning that year's Liege-Rome-Liege sports car rally, fighting off the likes of Porsche, Alfa Romeo, Austin Healey and Mini Cooper.

⸙ Canada Bound ⸙

Along with Carnaby Street fashions and the sound of the Beatles, an Austin Mini with a Union Jack paint scheme was chosen to represent modern Britain as part of James Gardner's design at Montreal's massive Expo '67 exhibition.

⸙ Learning from the Finns ⸙

When Timo Makinen and Rauno Aaltonen joined the BMC rally team, they brought with them a method of cornering that had been developed and perfected in Scandinavia. It had been honed on the front-wheel drive

Saab and would work equally well on the front-wheel drive Mini Cooper. The driver would kick hard at the brake pedal with his left foot while keeping his right foot pressed firmly down on the accelerator. Consequently the power of the engine would overcome and negate the front brakes while the rear brakes twitched the car sideways as it entered the corner, helpfully pointing it towards the exit. It was an excellent technique for getting out of trouble if entering a corner too fast, and it was one which Paddy Hopkirk soon picked up from his Finnish teachers.

❖ Italian Job Revisited ❖

For the 2003 remake of *The Italian Job*, the Minis of the original film were replaced by the new BMW-built MINI Cooper and MINI Cooper S, the classic Mini making only a cameo appearance. The film starred Mark Wahlberg and Donald Sutherland, but sadly not Minnie Driver.

❖ Anchors Aweigh… with the Fairies ❖

Tony Anchors, from Didcot, Oxfordshire, is a serial Mini customiser. Every year in the 1990s he dreamed up some new disguise for his old Mini. In 1992, he turned it into a two-seater Noddy car. Then there was Flower Power – a Mini modified to incorporate garden gates, window boxes with real flowers, garden gnomes, a fish pond and fountain. A Mississippi paddle steamer came next, but sadly that ended up at the bottom of a lake at the NEC in Birmingham. He created a Mini sandwich, a Mini thatched cottage and in 1997 a Mini garage, the car having its own built-on, fold-up garage.

In 1998, he unveiled one of his most ambitious projects to date – transforming his Mini into an open-topped, double-decker bus, complete with stairs to the top deck. Adapted with a box section steel frame and clad with timber boarding in a style loosely based on an old trolley bus, his Mini minibus took a week to build, was fitted with seat belts and complied with EC safety regulations.

He has even designed Mini-based furniture, including a two-piece suite from the front ends of three white Minis (with wheels), plus a standard lamp, drinks cabinet and coffee table all built from Mini parts.

In 2003, the father-of-four converted the car into a mobile Mini bar with faux brick walls, tiled roof and seating inside for five. 'The car is street legal,' he confirmed. 'My pals come for a drink in the drive or I go round to their place.'

His long-suffering wife Sharon sighed: 'He's as mad as a hatter.'

❖ Mini Rally Victories ❖

1962:   Tulip (Pat Moss)
        German (Pat Moss)
1963:   French Alpine (Rauno Aaltonen)
1964:   Monte Carlo (Paddy Hopkirk)
        Tulip (Timo Makinen)
1965:   Monte Carlo (Timo Makinen)
        Circuit of Ireland (Paddy Hopkirk)
        Geneva (Rauno Aaltonen)
        Czech (Rauno Aaltonen)
        Polish (Rauno Aaltonen)
        1,000 Lakes (Timo Makinen)
        Three Cities (Rauno Aaltonen)
        RAC (Rauno Aaltonen)
1966:   Circuit of Ireland (Tony Fall)
        Tulip (Rauno Aaltonen)
        Austrian Alpine (Paddy Hopkirk)
        Scottish (Tony Fall)
        Czech (Rauno Aaltonen)
        Polish (Tony Fall)
        1,000 Lakes (Timo Makinen)
        Three Cities (Timo Makinen)
1967:   Monte Carlo (Rauno Aaltonen)
        Circuit of Ireland (Paddy Hopkirk)
        Acropolis (Paddy Hopkirk)
        Geneva (Tony Fall)
        1,000 Lakes (Timo Makinen)
        French Alpine (Paddy Hopkirk)

❖ A Close Shave ❖

After the farce of the 1966 event, BMC were determined to see justice done by winning the 1967 Monte Carlo Rally, which they did, courtesy of Rauno Aaltonen. But it was a close-run thing, as the new competitions manager, Peter Browning, recalled: 'After the event the cars were taken apart by the scrutineers, and I remember a fat Frenchman holding the carbs in his hand looking at all the details. What he didn't know was that there was an illegal modification of a balance pipe between the carbs, but he didn't see it because he had his fat fingers over it! I nearly had a nervous breakdown, but we got away with it.'

❖ Rover's Return ❖

When Rover re-introduced the Mini Cooper in 1990 in the form of a 1,650-off special edition, John Cooper apparently thought that he would have to sign the bonnet of every single car!

❖ The Mini Moke ❖

First produced in the UK in 1964, the Mini Moke could climb a 1 in 2 gradient and was originally designed for the British Army but proved to have insufficient ground clearance for military use. BMC had hoped that the Moke would be classed as a commercial vehicle and would therefore not incur purchase tax, but instead it was deemed to be a car as it could carry passengers. Thus it was launched at a price of £405 in just one colour – Spruce Green. The only standard fitting was a windscreen wiper for the driver. Everything else was optional, including passenger seats, heater, grab handles, and a removable canvas top.

Mini Mokes have proved highly adaptable, being used as police cars in Barbados and Macau, beach buggies in Australia, the US and the Seychelles, and, with distinctive striped canopies, as taxis in the 1967 cult TV series *The Prisoner*, where their appearance did much to boost sales. In 1968, a team of Mokes equipped with roll bars and the Mini Cooper S 1275cc engine were entered in autocross grass track competitions by the John Player cigarette company.

A total of 14,518 Mokes were produced at Longbridge – 1,467 for home sales and 13,051 for export, mainly to hotter climes. In 1968, production of the Moke switched to Australia, from where it was exported to 82 countries. Customers included the Israeli Army who drove Mokes with machine gun tripods mounted in the rear. After 1981, as production in Australia wound down, the Moke was manufactured in Portugal.

In the early 1970s, the Mini Moke had the distinction of becoming the first motor vehicle to be driven on remote Pitcairn Island in the South Pacific. It was chosen because it was the only off-road vehicle that could be lifted by the island's solitary crane, there being no dock or airstrip on Pitcairn. Alas, the rough terrain and heavy rainfall proved too much even for the doughty little Moke and it soon broke down. However two more Mokes were eventually sent to the island and by using the other two for spares, the island's first vehicle remained running until at least 1988.

Mini Mokes have also featured in a number of films, including the Beatles' *Help!*, the Dave Clark Five's *Catch Us If You Can*, *Carry On Camping*, and the Bond movies *You Only Live Twice*, *The Spy Who Loved Me*, *Moonraker* and *Live and Let Die*.

Alec Issigonis went on to develop a Twini Moke, adding another engine in the back to go with the one in the front. The two engines – the front was 950cc, the rear 850cc – acted independently, each powering one set of wheels, the only connections between them being the throttle cables and gear levers. John Cooper tested it in heavy snow and found that he could 'drive as fast as he could see'.

❖ Mirror, Mirror ❖

As part of a 1998 exhibition called '40 Years of a Design Icon', David Bowie, who had owned a number of Minis in his time, designed his dream car – a Mini festooned with mirrors. Stunning though it looked, it was never intended for road use.

❖ Twin-Engined Mini ❖

Not content with a twin-engined Mini Moke, Alec Issigonis also contemplated a twin-engined Mini saloon. The idea of yet more power in a Mini inevitably caught the imagination of John Cooper who built a prototype model. BMC even entered a 2.5-litre Twini Mini – developing 175bhp – in the great Sicilian road race, the Targa Florio, where, driven by John Whitmore and Paul Frère, its superior speed in practice was offset by the rate at which it got through a set of tyres.

In the race itself, it burst its rear radiator on the start line and eventually lost so much water that the rear engine had to be disconnected. After that, it proved four seconds slower per lap than its single-engined counterpart.

In the end the Twini Mini project was cancelled after Cooper's car broke its steering while he was driving it at 100mph down the Kingston by-pass in Surrey. The car somersaulted into a wall, leaving Cooper with a fractured skull and a headache that would last him for the rest of his life.

⁘ Fond Memories ⁘

'I don't have any bad memories of the Mini compared to other cars I drove. If there was ever a problem with the Mini, we knew we would come back next time and win.' – Rauno Aaltonen

⁘ Minis Only! ⁘

First run in 1994, the Mini Europe Rally is a three-day navigational rally for Minis only. The brainchild of former Dutch rally drivers Gerrit Reinders and Harry Terpstra, it takes dozens of Minis through the heart of Europe.

⁘ Get Me to the Church ⁘

Except for a bride with a very modest train, a Mini would hardly be the ideal wedding day conveyance. But in 1985 a Lancashire-based company devised the Beauford, a Mini-based vehicle that was to prove extremely popular as wedding transport. Available in kit form, it consisted of a Mini body as the passenger compartment but the vehicle was adorned with a long bonnet and extravagant wings to give the appearance of a luxury car from the 1930s. Although it was a Mini at heart, it certainly didn't look like a Mini.

❖ A Four-Passenger Donkey! ❖

The word 'Moke' is a slang term for donkey, and US brochures actually read: 'Own a four-passenger donkey! The Austin Mini Moke is as tough and versatile as its namesake, but not half so obstinate. The rugged transverse-mounted BMC engine, combined with front-wheel drive, makes it sure-footed on the roughest terrain. Carrying a load, caddying around the golf course or coursing over back roads and beaches, the Austin Mini Moke is the real "can do" vehicle. A lot more economical than a donkey, too!'

❖ Birthday Party ❖

The Mini's thirtieth birthday party was held at Silverstone in August 1989. Over 37,000 Minis – some from as far away as Finland – converged on Northamptonshire, and 5,093 of them parked on the circuit, five abreast, to form a swarm of Minis that stretched for as far as the eye could see. The total public attendance for the weekend was 120,000, which was more than Silverstone attracted for the British Grand Prix meeting.

∹ Collectors' Items ∹

Miguel Plano, of Gatineau, Quebec, Canada, and his father Ricardo are mad about Minis, particularly models of Minis. Starting with two toy Minis in 1990 when he was eight years old, Miguel now has a collection of more than 850 model Minis from all over the world, including cars by Corgi, Dinky Toys and Hot Wheels. Among his prized possessions are Corgi replicas of the victorious Monte Carlo Rally cars of the 1960s.

∹ The Elf and the Hornet ∹

Seeking to take the Mini upmarket, BMC added two luxury models to the Mini range in 1961: the Riley Elf and the Wolseley Hornet. With extended rear wings and tail fins, the Elf and Hornet had extra boot space which made them eight and a half inches longer than the Mini. A recirculating heater, screenwashers, roof lamps and a wind-tone horn were standard, while a fresh-air heater was available as an extra. The seats were edged in leather, and both cars had wood-veneer dashboards, with the Elf's superior as befitted the more expensive car. They were powered by the basic 848cc A-Series engine, developing 34bhp. *Autocar* wrote: 'It is apparent from the specification that the Wolseley Hornet and Riley Elf will satisfy those small-car buyers who put a premium on finish and comprehensive equipment at the expense of some performance due to extra weight.'

The Mark II – with a more powerful 998cc engine giving 38bhp and a top speed of 78mph – was introduced in 1963, followed by a Mark III in 1966, but neither car in any of its forms caught the public's imagination in the same way as the Mini, and the Elf and Hornet were discontinued in 1969. Perhaps this was partly due to the fact that, when it first appeared in 1961, the Elf cost £574 10s 5d (including tax), making it around £80 more expensive than the Mini.

As prizes in a competition run by Heinz Soups, Crayford Engineering produced 57 convertible versions of the Hornet. Additional features in the Heinz Hornets included a fully equipped picnic case, an electric kettle and point in the boot, a 'ladies' freshen-up compartment' stocked with Max Factor products, and that essential item for every family picnic, a woollen tartan rug.

❖ Island Home ❖

There is an island off the coast of California where the Mini still reigns supreme. Catalina Island has strict regulations banning any vehicle over 10 feet (3 metres) in length, as a result of which the Mini has become the most popular car there. Graham Reid, proprietor of a Mini shop in Southern California, says: 'The rules are absolute, and nothing even slightly over 10 feet will get in. I even had a Clubman rejected once because its bumpers took it to 10 foot one. I had to re-bumper it.'

As the island gets more rainfall than the mainland, many residents choose a Mini in preference to a golf cart, although space is at such a premium that there is a ten-year waiting list to be allowed to own a car. There are believed to be around 14 Minis currently on the island, and among the lucky owners is Spencer Davis, leader of 1960s band the Spencer Davis Group. His Mini Cooper just keeps on running.

❖ The Rolls-Royce Mini ❖

Former Lotus engineer Brian Luff believed that Rolls-Royce owners were only really paying for the prestige of the grille. So for £20 he fitted a fibre-glass Roller bonnet and plastic grille to a standard Mini. He managed to sell about 80 of these luxury conversion kits in 1971 until Rolls-Royce Motors threatened legal action unless he called a halt to the joke.

❖ Woolly Mini ❖

For a 1971 fashion promotion, a Mini was covered in sheepskin and put on display outside Simpson's of Piccadilly, the renowned London menswear shop. To ensure maximum publicity, model Valerie Jane, wearing a pair of matching sheepskin hot pants, posed standing on the roof of the 'Wooli'.

❖ Issigonis Centenary ❖

To mark the centenary of the birth of Sir Alec Issigonis, hundreds of Minis attended a special gathering in 2006 at the Heritage Motor Centre, Gaydon. Among the myriad of Minis on display were an original 1959 Mini and a Moke towing a caravan made from plywood!

❖ Bushtucker Trial ❖

On a 2009 edition of ITV's *I'm a Celebrity... Get Me Out of Here,* former tennis ace Martina Navratilova took part in a Bushtucker Trial challenge that required her to clamber over a pontoon of five Minis suspended 10 metres above ground. However, the stunt upset Mini owners when the cars were then unceremoniously dropped into the water below. It was no way to treat a classic car.

❖ Rachel's Bottom ❖

After years of being teased about her curvy posterior, Rachel Brabbins, of Marlow, Buckinghamshire, bought the number plate BOT 70M for her Mini Cooper. A cat fan, Rachel has also put big white paw prints on the car roof.

❖ A Reflection of His Personality ❖

'His (Issigonis's) eyes, of a surprisingly intense deep blue, were recalled in the wide-eyed innocence of the Mini's headlights, childish but hugely sophisticated. The Mini was not only a triumph of engineering but an enduring personality, as was Sir Alec with his exquisitely caustic tongue and infectious merriment.'
– Sir Peter Ustinov, delivering the address at the funeral of Sir Alec Issigonis in 1988

❖ First Nine Finishers ❖

In the 1966 Bathurst 500-mile race for saloon cars in Australia, Mini Cooper S cars filled the first nine places.

Twenty-four of the 53 starters that year were Minis and it was car number 13, driven by Rauno Aaltonen and Bob Holden, that won in a time of 7hr 11min.

❖ Austin Ant ❖

Using Mini technology, Alec Issigonis developed the Austin Ant (one wag suggested that Ant stood for 'Alec's New Toy'), the first four-wheel-drive vehicle to have a transverse engine. It looked like a small Land Rover — it was only three inches (7.5cm) longer than the basic Mini — and could have been a big success with country dwellers but it only got as far as pre-production before being cancelled in 1968 by the new British Leyland regime. The reason was simple: BL owned Land Rover and perceived the Ant to be too similar. About 30 Ants were built in total.

❖ The Most Expensive Mini ❖

Sold for $80,000 (around £50,000 at the time), the Mini Limo, which was created as a one-off by John Cooper Garages for the 1997 Frankfurt Motor Show, was the most expensive Mini ever built. Interior features of the luxury show car included Wilton carpets, electric leather seats, a state-of-the-art stereo system, and satellite navigation.

❖ Hunt the Shunt ❖

At around the same time that the man who would become his great rival, Niki Lauda, was taking his first tentative steps in a Mini in Austria, James Hunt was leading something of a parallel existence in Britain. Both men were born into wealthy families, had little interest in education, and, to the dismay of their parents, just wanted to race. Hunt caught the bug after attending a club meeting at Silverstone on his eighteenth birthday, whereupon he suggested to his stockbroker father that he would be happy to accept the £2,500 that it would cost to send him to medical school as a one-off payment for his own use instead. Sensing that this would involve the purchase of a car to race, Hunt Senior declined the generous offer. Incidentally, Lauda's plan for acquiring funds had been altogether more devious. He persuaded a friend to forge him a college graduation certificate, and as a reward for their son's supposed academic achievements, his family promptly rewarded him with enough money to buy a car.

Strapped for cash, Hunt could only afford a ramshackle Mini, which he proceeded to rebuild in the family garage, financing the project by working in a series of jobs including labourer, hospital porter and van driver, the last proving useful for collecting parts for his car. By 1967, Hunt was ready to race, but unfortunately the scrutineers at Snetterton decided that his Mini wasn't. They took exception to the car's lack of a windscreen and the fact that the driver's seat was an old garden chair. When Hunt did finally make the starting grid, his makeshift Mini struggled as he continued to cut corners on and off the track. His habit of cutting grooves in bald tyres that he couldn't afford to replace, allied to a wild driving style, unsurprisingly resulted in a succession of crashes, earning him his nickname of 'Hunt the Shunt'.

❖ The Little Scamp ❖

When Leyland cancelled British production of the Moke in 1968, Robert Mandry, proprietor of the Connaught Garage, near Brookwood, Surrey, decided to build his own replacement. Without the benefit of any drawings on which to base his design, he quickly came up with the Scamp, and by 1969 he had a complete kit on the market. For £175, customers could buy a robust tubular chassis, clothed in aluminium sheet. For the more adventurous, there were vans, pickups, estates and even six-wheeled Scamps. Production of the Mark I Scamp ceased in 1978, having been declared illegal because the headlamps were too low, but the Mark II appeared shortly afterwards with bigger, 12-inch wheels and a hard-top with gull-wing doors, which bolted over the two seats and folding windscreen. The basic price was £385 for the body and about £150 for the hard-top.

Over 3,000 Scamps have been sold since 1969, mostly for off-road use, and with any number of optional extras available (soft tops, bull bars, wheelarch extensions, spare wheel carriers, tail-gated chassis, and a whole range of bumpers), it is reckoned that no two Scamps are the same.

⋙ Doh! A Simpsons Mini ⋘

Since 1997, Paul and Liz Halpine, from Thurnscoe, South Yorkshire, have built over 200 custom Minis. Their company, P & L Minis, has airbrushed Minis with pictures of characters from Warner Bros cartoons, *Wacky Races*, *Star Trek*, and, most recently *The Simpsons*. Their Simpsons Mini, which sold for £10,000, came complete with pictures of Marge, a burger-eating Homer and saxophone-playing Lisa on the passenger door, the US flag on the roof, and a graphic of Bart dropping his shorts on the boot lid.

❖ Turin Pilgrimage ❖

Over 100 Mini enthusiasts from all over Europe, the United States, New Zealand and Japan take their cars on an annual pilgrimage to Turin in an attempt to retrace the locations of *The Italian Job*. Organiser Freddie St. George says: 'We don't drive down the steps of the church though. During the original film, the directors just winged it. They did the stunt without getting local permission and apologised later.' The first run was in 1990 and the event has since raised more than £2 million for children's charities. Sir Michael Caine, star of the original film, is one of the event's patrons.

❖ Amphibious Minis ❖

Bizarre as it may sound, a Mini entered the 1977 River Severn Raft Race. Longbridge engineers converted a standard Mini into an unsinkable four-paddle-wheel-drive amphibious vehicle which they christened Aqua Min. However, it was not the first Mini to swim. Nine years earlier, an amphibious Moke swam in the River Thames for the Sammy Davis Jnr film *Salt and Pepper*. Since the movie was a James Bond spoof, it was only right that the Moke (registration SALT 1) should have machine guns fitted behind the headlights.

❖ Golden Year ❖

1965 was the year when the Mini swept all before it in competition. That year the Mini won a total of 17 international rallies and picked up no fewer than 116 major awards in international rallies and races. In addition to works victories in the Monte Carlo, the Circuit of Ireland, the Geneva, the Czech, the Polish, the 1,000 Lakes, the Three Cities and the RAC rallies, private Mini owners won the Basco-Navarrais, the Bodensee, the Saragossa, the Flowers and Perfumes, the Lorraine, the Armagnac, the Portuguese, and the Austrian Gold Cup rallies. Not surprisingly the first three places in the rally drivers' championship went to Mini men Rauno Aaltonen, Tony Ambrose and Timo Makinen. It was also the first time that the championship had been won in a British car.

❖ Ruffled Feathers ❖

'What John Cooper did with the Mini was quite extraordinary. It upset all the nice people who were racing in the British Championship in touring cars when the (Ford) Galaxy and 3.8 litre Jaguars were being made to look pretty silly by these little cars going sideways a fair amount of the time.' – Jackie Stewart

❖ The Great Escape ❖

During breaks in filming *The War Lover* at Shepperton Studios in late 1961 and early 1962, Steve McQueen used to indulge in his passion for motor racing. In an event at Brands Hatch he locked his Mini Cooper's brakes coming out of a fast turn in the wet, throwing the car sideways off the track and narrowly avoiding serious injury. A motoring correspondent described the incident: 'As he hurtled downhill off the road, McQueen did a superb job of propelling the Cooper between a series of poles and metal signs that could have demolished it. He controlled his slide until the final instant, looped, and slammed the car at an angle into a dirt embankment. The Cooper snapped around like a top, whirling and bouncing, but miraculously did not turn over.' Even so McQueen had to wear an oxygen mask for the next day's filming to hide his swollen lip and scratched face.

McQueen's impressive collection of cars later included a 1967 Mini Cooper S. Originally in British Racing Green, the car was customised soon after McQueen bought it. It was repainted brown, a sunroof was added and because he didn't like to look at a radio antenna while he was driving, he had it moved into a recess in the right rear wing. One night he was driving the car through the Hollywood Hills when he suddenly needed to answer a call of nature. Since it was dark, he pulled to the side of the road, parked and jumped out. Unfortunately he had forgotten to put the handbrake on and while he was in the middle of his pee, he watched as the car gently rolled past.

❖ Tribute Band ❖

In 1999, Welsh band Stereophonics did their own spoof version of the chase scenes in *The Italian Job*, being seen at the wheels of Austin Mini Coopers for the video of their single 'Pick A Part That's New'.

❖ Mini Designer ❖

Launched in 1988 at a price of £4,654, the special edition Mini Designer was designed by Mary Quant, pioneer of that other great mini that epitomised the Swinging Sixties, the mini skirt. The car had black and white striped seats, Quant's signature on the front seats and her 'daisy' motif on the centre of the steering wheel.

❖ Spirit of Adventure ❖

That same spirit of adventure which characterises the original Minis has been retained by owners of the new BMW MINIs. Each year since 2003, some 250 owners drive their MINIs to the 6,288ft summit of Mount Washington, New Hampshire, for the MINIs On Top parade.

❖ The Marples Hatchback ❖

In the early 1960s, the Austin Experimental Department built three Mini Cooper S hatchbacks, but the car was never put into production. In 1968, one of the trio – a 1964 Austin Cooper S 1071cc hatchback – was bought by Ernest Marples, the controversial Conservative Minister of Transport from 1959 to 1964. The Marples Hatchback, as it has become known, is now a collectors' item and was recently put up for sale at around £20,000.

❖ The Car that Never Was ❖

Between 1967 and 1970, Alec Issigonis worked on designing a replacement for the Mini – an experimental model called the 9X. Due to its rushed development, the Mini suffered from a number of compromises (although in time enthusiasts came to view these as loveable eccentricities) and Issigonis was keen to develop a replacement that would not be hampered in the same way.

At just 9ft 8in (2.9m) long, the 9X was shorter than the Mini but its squarer shape gave it greater head and leg room. It was also more powerful than the Mini, the 1-litre engine of the prototype giving 60bhp, compared to the 40bhp of the 998cc Mini. With its advanced technology, many motoring experts believe the 9X would have been competitive well into the 1980s but due to internal politicking within British Leyland, the car was never built.

Some of the 9X engines were used in standard Minis as part of their development, and shortly after the 9X was scrapped, one of these cars was lent to a British Leyland director. He returned from a test drive enthusing about how well the Mini went with its new engine and suggested it should be offered for sale. Imagine his reaction when he looked under the bonnet and realised that it was the very engine that he had just consigned to the scrapheap.

⁘ The Oldest Mini ⁘

The first Mini off the Cowley production line – a white model registration 621 AOK – currently has pride of place at the Heritage Motor Centre in Gaydon, Warwickshire. Other exhibits there include the red and white Mini Cooper, 33 EJB, in which Paddy Hopkirk and co-driver Henry Liddon won the 1964 Monte Carlo Rally.

❖ Bibliography ❖

The Beaulieu Encyclopedia of the Automobile – ed. Nick Georgano (The Stationery Office, 2000)

Issigonis – Gillian Bardsley (Icon Books, 2005)

Men and Motors of the Austin – Barney Sharratt (Haynes, 2000)

Mini – James Ruppert (Crowood Press, 1997)

The Mini: A Celebration – Graham Scott (Hamlyn, 1992)

Mini: A Celebration of Britain's Best-Loved Small Car – Graham Robson (Haynes, 2006)

The Mini: 40 Years of Fun – Brian Laban (HarperCollins, 1999)

Mini Purchase and Restoration Guide – Lindsay Porter (Foulis, 1996)

Mini: The Design Icon of a Generation – L.J.K. Setright (Virgin, 1999)

Mini: Thirty-Five Years On – Rob Golding (Osprey, 1994)
❖ Bibliography ❖

❖ Other Titles in this Series ❖

The Boxing Miscellany

The Celtic Football Miscellany

The England Cricket Miscellany

The England Football Miscellany

The Formula One Miscellany

The Golf Miscellany

The Horse Racing Miscellany

The Liverpool Football Miscellany

The Olympic Miscellany

The Premiership Football Miscellany

The Rangers Football Miscellany

The Six Nations Rugby Miscellany

The United Miscellany